Making Sense
of the Trinity

3 Crucial Questions
Grant R. Osborne and Richard J. Jones, Jr., editors

Other books by Millard J. Erickson (selected)

Making Sense of the Trinity

3 Crucial Questions

Millard J. Erickson

Baker Books

A Division of Baker Book House Co
Grand Rapids, Michigan 49516

© 2000 by Millard J. Erickson

Published by Baker Books
a division of Baker Book House Company
P.O. Box 6287, Grand Rapids, MI 49516–6287

Printed in the United States of America

Library of Congress Cataloging-in-Publication Data is on file at the Library of Congress, Washington, D.C.

For information about academic books, resources for Christian leaders, and all new releases available from Baker Book House, visit our web site:
http://www.bakerbooks.com

Contents

Editors' Preface

The books in the 3 Crucial Questions series are the published form of the 3 Crucial Questions Seminars, which are sponsored by Bridge Ministries of Detroit, Michigan. The seminars and books are designed to greatly enhance your Christian walk. The following comments will help you appreciate the unique features of the book series.

The 3 Crucial Questions series is based on two fundamental observations. First, there are crucial questions related to the Christian faith for which imperfect Christians seem to have no final answers. Christians living in eternal glory may know fully even as they are known by God, but now we know only in part (1 Cor. 13:12). Therefore, we must ever return to such questions with the prayer that God the Holy Spirit will continue to lead us nearer to "the truth, the whole truth, and nothing but the truth." While recognizing their own frailty, the authors contributing to this series pray that they are thus led.

Second, each Christian generation partly affirms its solidarity with the Christian past by reaffirming "the faith which was once delivered unto the saints" (Jude 3 KJV). Such an affirmation is usually attempted by religious scholars who are notorious for talking only to themselves or by nonexperts whose grasp of the faith lacks depth of insight. Both situations are unfortunate, but we feel that our team of contributing authors is well prepared to avoid them. Each author is a competent Christian scholar able to share tremendous learning in down-to-earth language both laity and experts can appreciate. In a word, you have in hand a book that is part of a rare series, one that is neither pedantic nor pediatric.

The topics addressed in the series have been chosen for their timelessness, interest level, and importance to Christians everywhere. And the contributing authors are committed to discussing them in a manner that promotes Christian unity. Thus, they discuss not only areas of disagreement among Christians but significant areas of agreement as well. Seeking peace and pursuing it as the Bible commands (1 Peter 3:11), they stress common ground on which Christians with different views may meet for wholesome dialogue and reconciliation.

The books in the series consist not merely of printed words; they consist of words to live by. Their pages are filled not only with good information but with sound instruction in successful Christian living. For study is truly Christian only when, in addition to helping us understand our faith, it helps us to live our faith. We pray therefore that you will allow God to use the 3 Crucial Questions series to augment your growth in the grace and knowledge of our Lord and Savior Jesus Christ.

Grant R. Osborne

Author's Preface

The doctrine of the Trinity has always been a puzzle to Christians. For that reason, some have rejected this unique teaching. Yet it lies at the very heart of the Christian faith.

I continue to be impressed by the amount of interest in doctrine in general and in the Trinity in particular. This was confirmed to me during a weekend theological conference based on the three chapters of this book, held at First Covenant Church, Omaha, Nebraska, on September 28–29, 1997. The questions and comments from those who attended were of great help to me in further developing those topics. I am grateful to Dr. Al Jackson and pastors Philip Haakenson and John Larson for that invitation.

I also appreciate the invitation from Dr. Grant Osborne and Rev. Richard Jones, to contribute this book to the Three Crucial Questions series. Although the lectures that were to be given on these topics were canceled when Bridge Ministries closed, Baker Book House has graciously consented to publish this manuscript nonetheless. Maria denBoer has edited the manuscript with her usual skill.

These topics have been developed in keeping with the type of audience described above in mind. Those who are interested in a more advanced and technical treatment of the questions are referred to my *God in Three Persons* (Baker, 1995).

In memory of Herman Baker, 1911–1991
Founder and President, Baker Book House, 1939–1987
Lover of God
Lover of Books

Introduction

To those outside the Christian faith, the doctrine of the Trinity seems a very strange teaching indeed. It seems to violate logic, for it claims that God is three and yet that he is one. How can this be? And why would the church propound such a doctrine? It does not appear to be taught in Scripture, which is the Christian's supreme authority in matters of faith and practice. And it presents an obstacle to faith for those who otherwise might be inclined to accept the Christian faith. Is it a teaching that perhaps was a mistake in the first place, and certainly is a hindrance and an embarrassment to Christianity? Could it be omitted from Christian faith and theology, without any loss and even with considerable gain? I submit that the doctrine of the Trinity is of great importance in our time, and therefore needs to be examined carefully, for several reasons.

First, this doctrine historically was the first that the church felt it necessary to elaborate in a definitive fashion. The church began preaching its message, which entailed the deity of Jesus as well as that of the Father. It had not thoroughly worked out the nature of the relationship between these two persons, however. Christians simply assumed that both were God. Soon some persons began to raise questions regarding just what this meant. The proposals they made in attempting to give some concrete content did not sound totally correct to many Christians, however, so a more complete explanation was worked out. This became the full doctrine of the Trinity, that all three, Father, Son, and Holy Spirit, are divine, but that they are not three

Gods, but one. It was deemed essential to the life of the church
to hold this doctrine of God's three-in-oneness.

It was not simply the church of the third and fourth centuries
that encountered challenges to this view. Although more than
fifteen centuries have gone by since the church took its stand,
there are still varieties of Christianity that deny the Trinity. This
is still very much an issue in our time, as groups such as the
Jehovah's Witnesses dispute the full deity of Jesus and thus the
doctrine of the Trinity. Numerous cults and sects reject this view,
as do some liberal Christians within better known Christian
denominations.

The doctrine is also particularly important at a time when we
are encountering many different religions. At one time the
choice for a person living in the Western Hemisphere was either
Christianity or no religion, unless that person was a Native American. There really were no other viable alternatives. Other religions were somewhere far removed, in other countries. The one
exception to this was Judaism, but it was generally regarded as
a cultural and thus rather exclusive religion. All has changed
today, however. Currently, Muslims outnumber Episcopalians
in the United States, and their relative numbers are growing.[1]
Islam is Christianity's major religious competitor for the alle-
giance of young African-American males. Note the number of
professional athletes who now bear Islamic names, such as
Muhammad Ali, Kareem Abdul-Jabbar, Ahmad Rashad, and
many others, particularly basketball players. These young men
who are becoming conscious of and asserting their African her-
itage are often told that Christianity is a white man's religion;
Islam is the true religion of Africans. Buddhist and Hindu houses
of worship can be found in every major city. New Age religion,
which incorporates many features of Eastern religions, is a growing option for many younger persons.

The doctrine of the Trinity is a major distinguishing feature
of Christianity which sets it apart from these other religions. On
the one hand, it clearly distinguishes Christianity from the
strongly monotheistic religions such as Judaism and Islam. On

the other hand, it separates Christianity from polytheistic and pantheistic religions such as the Eastern religions. Thus, it is especially important in our time.

The doctrine of the Trinity is also of great importance because it is intimately connected with the Christian's salvation. Traditionally, Christians have believed that salvation, involving forgiveness of sin and reception of new life, is possible because the second person of the Godhead took on human form without giving up his deity. In this incarnate form he bore the sins of humans as their substitute. Thus he was able to present to the Father the perfect sacrifice for human sin, on the basis of which the Father then forgave their sins and the Holy Spirit conferred new life. If the doctrine of the Trinity is not true, then the understanding of salvation must be modified.

Further, our view on this doctrine affects our views of other doctrines. If the Godhead does not consist of three persons equally divine and yet inseparably one, we must redefine one or more of those persons. Jesus may not be fully God, or if he is, he is a lesser deity than is the Father. The Holy Spirit is in some sense inferior to both the Father and the Son. The doctrine of the atonement is modified as well. Instead of a voluntary self-sacrifice by a member of the Godhead, it is something imposed on a human by God, and thus contains an element of injustice.

What, then, shall we say about the doctrine of the Trinity? While those who give special authority to church councils have their authoritative answer, that answer does not necessarily suffice for those Christians who do not consider the pronouncements of church councils infallible. And even those who do must reckon with the fact that those declarations were made in a very different age, using language and concepts that may not make sense to twentieth- and twenty-first-century persons. For some, the doctrine of the Trinity is a stumbling-block to belief. Can any help be offered to them?

Three questions in particular require our attention. The first concerns the biblical status of the doctrine. This teaching does not seem to be stated in the Bible. Is it taught there? If not, perhaps the church was mistaken in formulating such a strange teaching. We must look closely at the biblical testimony to determine whether this doctrine is indeed found there.

The second question pertains to the logical status of this doctrine. If God is three and yet is one, we are facing an apparent logical contradiction. If the Bible requires us to hold this view, is there some way to understand it that will remove this puzzle, or at least soften it enough so that we are not forced to abandon our rationality in order to be Trinitarians? A number of explanations have been attempted, and we will examine them and seek to find the most satisfying.

The final question is one that I was taught to ask of any proposal: "So what?" What real difference does it make if this doctrine is true? Does it actually have an impact on the way we live our Christian lives, or is it simply an impractical and thus unnecessary element in Christian theology? We will seek to weigh all of the ramifications of this teaching.

Is the Doctrine
of the Trinity Biblical?

We have noted that the church formulated the strange doctrine of the Trinity because it felt compelled, on the basis of its study of Scripture, to affirm both that God is one and that there are three who are God. It did this through the doctrine of triunity: that God is three in one.

It is important, then, that we reexamine the evidence that they followed, since the conclusions drawn from it are under challenge, even attack, today. In evangelical circles, it is customary to affirm that the Bible is the supreme authority for faith and practice, or even the sole authority. Even where this is not so completely or officially the case, Christians certainly consider it important. All would recognize the Bible as in some sense, the Christian book, the source of Christian belief. If, then, this strange-appearing doctrine is taught in the Bible, either explicitly or implicitly, we must accept it, or at least take it very seriously.

If, on the other hand, the Bible does not assert such a teaching, we may not be required to believe it. Ideas which were actually derived from misunderstandings of the text or from cultural sources, have, of course, been adopted by individual Christians or even the church as a whole at various points in its history.

There is no virtue in continuing to hold such a difficult doctrine
of the Trinity if it is not actually taught in the Bible.

The church, we noted earlier, drew the inference of the Trinity from two sets of evidence it accepted. On the one hand, the
Bible taught that God is one. On the other, there were three
persons whom the Bible seemed to identify as being divine.

The Unity of God

The reality that there is only one God is both taught and presupposed throughout Scripture. Probably the clearest and most
direct teaching is the well-known Shema in Deuteronomy 6:4:
"Hear, O Israel: The LORD our God, the LORD is one." This was
the basis of the command that followed: "Love the LORD your
God with all your heart and with all your soul and with all your
strength" (v. 5). Because Jehovah was the only God and there
was no other, Israel was not to divide their loyalty for him with
any other claimed deities. Monotheism means exclusive worship of and obedience to the one true God.

This same exclusiveness appears as well in the Ten Com-
mandments. Here Jehovah asserts that he is God, the true God,
who brought the Israelites out of the land of Egypt. The prohibition of making any sort of graven image is based, again, on the
fact that there are no other gods, so worship of anything other
than Jehovah is idolatry. Although the teaching of God's oneness does not reappear in the Old Testament, the continued
prohibition of worship of other gods and the necessity of worshiping Jehovah alone rest on that fact.

The teaching regarding God's oneness is not restricted to the
Old Testament. James 2:19 commends belief in one God, while
noting its insufficiency for justification. Paul also underscores
God's uniqueness. As he discusses the eating of meat that had
been offered to idols, the apostle writes: "We know that an idol
is nothing at all in the world and that there is no God but one
. . . the Father, from whom all things came and for whom we
live; and there is but one Lord, Jesus Christ, through whom all
things came and through whom we live" (1 Cor. 8:4, 6). Here

Paul, like the Mosaic law, excludes idolatry on the grounds that there is only one God. Similarly, he writes to Timothy: "For there is one God and one mediator between God and men, the man Christ Jesus, who gave himself as a ransom for all men" (1 Tim. 2:5–6). While on the surface these verses seem to distinguish Jesus from the only God, the Father, the primary thrust of the former reference is that God alone is truly God (idols are nothing); and the primary thrust of the latter is that there is but one God, and that there is only one mediator between God and humans.

The Deity of the Three

The considerations just noted, if taken alone, would have led the church to a simple monotheism. It was the additional conclusion, that three are identified in Scripture as being divine, that led to the adoption of the doctrine of the Trinity.

The Deity of the Father. The deity of the Father was scarcely in question. We noted above Paul's reference to the Father as the one God. Jesus also makes several references to the deity of the Father. For example, in Matthew 6:26–30, he uses "God" and "the Father" interchangeably. He says, "your heavenly Father feeds [the birds of the air]" (v. 26) and "God clothes the grass of the field" (v. 30). And in verses 31–32 he states that we need not ask what we shall eat or drink or wear because "your heavenly Father knows that you need them." Similar expressions appear throughout his teachings. For Jesus, "God" and "your heavenly Father" are interchangeable expressions. And in numerous other references to God, Jesus obviously has the Father in mind (e.g., Matt. 19:23–26; 27:46; Mark 12:17, 24–27).

The Deity of Jesus. While the majority of biblical references bearing on the issue of Jesus' deity are in the New Testament, the Old Testament is not devoid of relevant data. These are especially found in the prophetic portions of the Old Testament. Although there was an anticipation of a great messiah and deliverer, this did not necessarily involve the idea of deity. In Isaiah

9:6, however, the prophet, referring to the one who was to come, wrote, "For to us a child is born, to us a son is given, and the government will be on his shoulders. And he will be called Wonderful Counselor, Mighty God, Everlasting Father, Prince of Peace." Here is an apparent identification of the coming messiah as "mighty God."

The New Testament contains abundant indications of the deity of Jesus. Philippians 2:5–11 is a powerful passage. In verse 6, Paul says of Jesus that "being in very nature God, [he] did not consider equality with God something to be grasped." The word translated "in very nature," or "in the form of," is the Greek *morphē*. It is the word that refers to the full set of characteristics which make something that which it is, as contrasted with the word *schēma,* which is the external appearance, or facade, which does not necessarily indicate the true nature of the thing.

The writer to the Hebrews also gives forceful expression to Jesus' deity. Writing to Hebrew readers, he speaks of the superiority of Jesus to angels, and indicates that God has spoken through him, made him the heir of all things, and created the universe through him (Heb. 1:2). Then he says, "The Son is the radiance of God's glory and the exact representation of his being, sustaining all things by his powerful word" (v. 3). The Greek word translated "exact representation" is *charaktēr,* from which our word, "character," is obviously derived. This is not merely similarity of being, but qualitative identity. Then in verse 8 the writer quotes God (from Ps. 45:6) as addressing the Son as "God" and in verse 10 as "Lord" (from Ps. 102:25).

Jesus' own self-understanding is important. The grandiose statements he made indicate either some strange delusion or that he is actually God. He claimed that God's angels (Luke 12:8–9; 15:10) were his angels (Matt. 13:41), and that God's kingdom was his (Matt. 12:28; 19:14, 24; 21:31, 43). God's elect were also his elect (Matt. 12:28; 19:14, 24; 21:31, 43). He also applied a number of Old Testament references to God to himself. The judgment scene of Matthew 25 reflects the theophanic language of Daniel 7:9–10, Joel 3:1–12, and Zechariah 14:5. In Matthew 21:16, Jesus applies Psalm 8:1–2 to himself, and in Luke 19:10 apparently alludes to Ezekiel 34:16, 22. Other references of this type are Luke 20:18a (Isa. 8:14–15); Matthew 11:10, Mark 1:2, and Luke 7:27 (Mal. 3:1; 4:5–6); Mark 13:31 (Isa. 40:8). There also are those passages in which he assumes the role of Yahweh. Among the most impressive of these are the predictions of the second coming and judgment. In Mark 9:12–13 (Matt. 17:11–12), Matthew 11:10 (Luke 7:27), and Matthew 11:14, there are references to Malachi 3:1 and 4:5–6, which predict the coming of Elijah as the forerunner of Yahweh. Jesus, however, identified John the Baptist, who had come as his forerunner, as Elijah. In Matthew 19:28 and 25:31–46, Jesus alludes to Daniel 7. In Daniel 7:9 the Ancient of Days sits on a throne. Jesus himself, however, takes the role of the Ancient of Days, sitting on his "glorious throne." And in parables where Jesus identifies himself as the sower, the shepherd, and the bridegroom, he places himself in the role of God.

Furthermore, the actions that Jesus claimed to perform, either currently or in the future, identify more completely this divine self-image. He claimed the power to judge the world (Matt. 25:31) and to reign over it (Matt. 24:30; Mark 14:62). Most significantly, however, he claimed to forgive sins (Mark 2:8–10). This was interpreted by the scribes and Pharisees as blasphemy, because it was something only God has the right and power to do. In fact, Jesus forgave sins knowing full well the interpretation the Jews would place on his action. In Mark 2:7 they say, "Why does this fellow talk like that? He's blaspheming! Who can forgive sins but God alone?" Jesus responds by word and action, "'But that you may know that the Son of Man has authority on earth to forgive sins . . .' He said to the paralytic, 'I tell you, get up, take your mat and go home'" (vv. 10–11). Thus, he deliberately acted in a way that he knew they would interpret his actions as claiming equality with God.

Even the expressions that Jesus used indicate his deity. One of the most important of these was, "But I say to you." This was introduced in connection with a quotation from the Old Testament Scriptures. In effect, he was saying, "Moses said that, but I say this to you." He was implicitly claiming the right or authority to supplement what they had learned from Moses, the one they regarded as having been God's special spokesperson. Note, however, the way Jesus reported these statements. He did not use the customary prophetic introduction, "The Word of the Lord came to me, saying . . ." Rather, he simply said, "I say to you." He did not claim to be reporting the message God had revealed to him. He was claiming that his words were God's words. Another expression that he used frequently was "Amen." In these instances the word is usually translated, "Truly, truly," or in the older versions, "Verily, verily." This expression was customarily used by the congregation of Israel in response to the Word of God, as a way of indicating their agreement, or acknowledging that this was God's message. For Jesus to use it in connection with his own words was a claim that his words were of equal status to those of the Old Testament messengers.

Nowhere did Jesus ever say overtly, "I am God." The closest he came to this was in connection with his trial. Here he was challenged, point-blank, "Tell us if you are the Christ, the Son of God," and he responded, "Yes, it is as you say. But I say to all of you: In the future you will see the Son of Man sitting at the right hand of the Mighty One and coming on the clouds of heaven" (Matt. 26:63–65). Some have claimed that Jesus' response was actually a disavowal, "You said it, not I," an interpretation that would be supported by the emphatic "you," but the reaction of the high priest and the others who were present indicates that they understood him quite differently: "Then the high priest tore his clothes and said, 'He has spoken blasphemy! Why do we need any more witnesses? Look, now you have heard the blasphemy. What do you think?' 'He is worthy of death,' they answered" (Matt. 26:63–65). If this was a false charge, Jesus had the ideal opportunity to disclaim it. Either he was deliberately seeking his own execution, even on false grounds, or he really did believe that he was the Son of God. And, when

Thomas exclaimed, "My Lord and my God!" (John 20:28), Jesus did not correct, but rather accepted, this tribute.

We have introduced the Gospel of John, and probably need to offer some justification for doing so. For some time, it was fashionable to consider John's Gospel historically unreliable. There were a number of reasons for this hesitancy. One is the very different way John's Gospel treats various materials in comparison to the Synoptics. He gives a great deal of attention to the events of the last days of Jesus' life before the crucifixion. His selection of materials is quite different as well, in terms of both inclusion and omission. Some events that are prominent in the Synoptics, such as the commissioning of the twelve apostles, the transfiguration, the institution of the Lord's Supper, the exorcisms, and the parables, do not appear. On the other hand, John includes a number of accounts which do not appear in any of the other Gospels, such as the transformation of water into wine, the raising of Lazarus, Jesus' early ministry in Judea and Samaria, and his extended discourses, both in public and in private. Further, John is the most theological of the Gospel writers, being the only evangelist to identify Jesus as divine. There are major chronological differences from the Synoptics, such as the length of Jesus' ministry and the chronology of the last twenty-four hours of Jesus' life. There seem to be historical discrepancies, such as John being apparently unaware of the birth in Bethlehem. Finally, there is the difficulty of distinguishing Jesus' words from John's interpretation of them.

A change in attitude of New Testament scholars toward John's Gospel began to become apparent in the 1960s, although it had been anticipated by some as early as the 1930s.[1] These different attitudes arose in some rather surprising places. Bishop John A. T. Robinson, of *Honest to God* fame, was the leading voice in this new movement toward increased trust in this Gospel.

A number of factors, both negative and positive, have been involved in this transformation of the estimate of the historical value of John's Gospel. Some of the problems and discrepancies have turned out not to be as severe as was once thought.

The alleged discrepancies, for example, can be viewed more as complementary than contradictory.[2] The theological differences also can be understood as John making explicit what was implicit in the other Gospels.[3] Further, the apparent chronological discrepancies become less significant when one realizes that the Synoptics really show little interest in chronology, and they do not limit the ministry to one year; they simply do not refer to three Passovers, as does John. The more extended period fits better with the events reported as part of Jesus' ministry, thus suggesting that John's chronology is less problematic than that of the Synoptics. The seeming historical discrepancies are less serious than first appears to be the case as well. John only reports, rather than affirms, the erroneous belief that Jesus had been born in Galilee. And the stylistic differences from the Synoptics, when examined in light of John's purposes, become less problematic.[4]

In addition to these responses to the criticisms, there also has been a considerable amount of positive evidence for the historical reliability of John's Gospel. One element was the revised view of the background of the Gospel. It was customary to regard John as a thoroughly Hellenistic Gospel. A number of factors have combined to undercut this supposed consensus, however. A major one was the discovery of the Dead Sea Scrolls. There are some strong parallels between the language and terminology of these documents and John's Gospel, but also and more important, between their ideas.[5]

There has also been archaeological confirmation of a number of topographical references in John. Robinson sees these extensive references as evidence of the historical reliability of the Gospel. It is especially informative to compare John's references to those of Luke. Luke, of course, is known for very precise references when dealing with familiar territory, such as is involved in the Book of Acts. In the chapters of his Gospel that deal with the Galilean ministry and in the long central portion from 9:51 to 18:14, however, Luke is quite vague. Compared with this, John is very precise in a number of instances.

Note, for example, 11:1–12:1, where John names the place, explains that it is about two miles from Jerusalem, tells us why Jesus went there on two occasions, from where, and in the second instance, exactly when—six days before the Passover. Recent archaeological study has tended to support the view that this Gospel was written by someone who knew well the places in which the story is set.[6]

It was customary to regard John's Gospel as being dependent on the Synoptics. C. H. Dodd argued both positively and negatively, however, for the independence of John from the Synoptics. He carefully examined the passages where John refers to an incident also mentioned in the Synoptics, and compares them carefully. In each case, he concludes that it is unlikely that John would have extracted just those details and combined them in just the way that he did. He also compiled a list of the types of statements one would expect to find if John had been utilizing the Synoptics as a source. Among them are references that fit well with John's symbolism, style, and purpose in writing, including such matters in the Gospel of Mark as the darkness at the crucifixion, the rending of the temple veil, and the confession by the centurion that Jesus was the Son of God. These are not present in John's account, however. This is for Dodd confirming evidence of John's independence from the Synoptics, and thus of his use of a separate historical source, which may well have been as reliable as, or more reliable than, the sources of the Synoptics.[7] Actually, it appears that John was being faulted both for his dependence on the Synoptics and for the differences between his writing and theirs.

One other factor bearing on the historical reliability of John's Gospel is the whole matter of the dating of the Gospels. It was fashionable at one time to date the Fourth Gospel well into the second century. The discovery of the John Rylands fragment of that Gospel pushed the date back to the latter part of the first century, so that it became customary to date all of the Johannine literature in the A.D. 90s.

Here, also, John Robinson began to raise the question of whether John's Gospel might not date from before the Jewish revolt of A.D. 66–70. This in turn would require on the standard theory of priority that the Synoptics be dated even earlier. One major consideration for Robinson was the absence of any reference in any of the Gospels to the fall of Jerusalem in A.D. 70, an event of such significance that it surely should have been referred to in any Gospel account. In view of such items as Jesus' statement about the stones being cast down, Mark 13:1–4 does not reflect the detail that should have been present if the event had already occurred.[8]

The Deity of the Holy Spirit. Belief in the deity of the Holy Spirit was not officially enunciated by the church until relatively late. The Council of Nicea, for example, after spelling out rather clearly the full deity of Jesus, concludes by saying simply, "[We believe] in the Holy Spirit," without specifying the content of that belief. By the Council of Constantinople in 381, however, this had been elaborated to the point where the church also committed itself to the deity of the Holy Spirit. The deity of the Holy Spirit is even less directly taught in Scripture than is the deity of the Father or the Son. There are, however, several considerations on the basis of which we may infer his deity as well.

There are various references to the Holy Spirit that are interchangeable with references to God, thus in effect speaking of him as God. In Acts 5 Ananias and Sapphira had sold a piece of property and represented the money they brought as the whole of what they had received. In rebuking Ananias, Peter asked, "Ananias, how is it that Satan has so filled your heart that you have lied to the Holy Spirit and have kept for yourself some of the money you received for the land?" (v. 3). In the next verse he asserts, "You have not lied to men but to God." It seems that in Peter's mind "lying to the Holy Spirit" and "lying to God" were interchangeable expressions. The statement in verse 4 was apparently intended to make clear that the lie was told not to humans, to someone less than God, but to God himself. Thus, we conclude that the second statement is an elaboration of the first, emphasizing that the Spirit to whom Ananias had lied was God.

Another passage where "Holy Spirit" and "God" are used interchangeably is Paul's discussion of the Christian as a temple. In 1 Corinthians 3:16–17 he writes, "Don't you know that you yourselves are God's temple and that God's Spirit lives in you? If anyone destroys God's temple, God will destroy him; for God's temple is sacred, and you are that temple." In 6:19–20 he uses almost identical language: "Do you not know that your body is a temple of the Holy Spirit, who is in you, whom you have received from God? You are not your own; you were bought at a price. Therefore honor God with your body." To Paul, to be indwelt by the Holy Spirit is to be inhabited by God. By equating the phrase "God's temple" with the phrase "a temple of the Holy Spirit," Paul makes it clear that the Holy Spirit is God.

Further, the Holy Spirit possesses the attributes or qualities of God. One of these is omniscience: "The Spirit searches all things, even the deep things of God. For who among men knows the thoughts of a man except the man's spirit within him? In the same way no one knows the thoughts of God except the Spirit of God" (1 Cor. 2:10–11). Also observe Jesus' statement in John 16:13: "When he, the Spirit of truth comes, he will guide you into all truth. He will not speak on his own; he will speak only what he hears, and he will tell you what is yet to come."

The New Testament writers also speak of the power of the Holy Spirit. In Luke 1:35 the phrases "the Holy Spirit" and "the power of the Most High" are in parallel or synonymous construction. This is, of course, a reference to the virginal conception, which must certainly be considered a miracle of the first magnitude. Paul acknowledged that the accomplishments of his ministry were achieved "by the power of signs and wonders, through the power of the Spirit" (Rom. 15:19). Moreover, Jesus attributed to the Holy Spirit the ability to change human hearts and personalities: it is the Spirit who works conviction (John 16:8–11) and regeneration (John 3:5–8) within us. Elsewhere he had said with respect to this ability to change human hearts: "With man this is impossible, but with God all things are possible" (Matt. 19:26; see vv. 16–25). While these texts do not specifically affirm that the Spirit is omnipotent, they certainly indicate that he has power which presumably only God has.

Yet another attribute of the Spirit which brackets him with the Father and the Son is his eternality. In Hebrews 9:14 he is spoken of as "the eternal Spirit" through whom Jesus offered himself up. All creatures are temporal; only God is eternal (Heb. 1:10–12). So the Holy Spirit must be God.

In addition to having divine attributes, the Holy Spirit performs certain works that are commonly ascribed to God. He was and continues to be involved with the creation, in both originating and providentially keeping and directing it. In Genesis 1:2 we read that the Spirit of God was brooding over the face of the waters. Job 26:13 notes that the heavens were made fair by the Spirit of God. The psalmist says, "When you send your Spirit, they [all the parts of the creation previously enumerated] are created, and you renew the face of the earth" (Ps. 104:30).

The most abundant biblical testimony regarding the role of the Holy Spirit concerns his spiritual working on or within humans. We have already noted Jesus' attribution of regeneration to the Holy Spirit (John 3:5–8). This is confirmed by Paul's statement in Titus 3:5: "[God our Savior] saved us, not because of righteous things we had done, but because of his mercy. He saved us through the washing of rebirth and renewal by the Holy Spirit." In addition, the Spirit raised Christ from the dead and will also raise us; that is, God will raise us through the Spirit: "If the Spirit of him who raised Jesus from the dead is living in you, he who raised Christ from the dead will give life to your mortal bodies also through his Spirit which dwells in you" (Rom. 8:11).

Giving the Scriptures is another divine work of the Holy Spirit. In 2 Timothy 3:16 Paul writes, "All Scripture is God-breathed and is useful for teaching, rebuking, correcting, and training in righteousness." Peter also speaks of the Spirit's role in giving us the Scriptures, but emphasizes the influence on the writer rather than the end product: "prophecy never had its origin in the will of man, but men spoke from God as they were carried along by the Holy Spirit" (2 Peter 1:21).

One question which deserves attention is the status of the Holy Spirit in the Old Testament references. Here the usual form of expression is "the Spirit of God" or "the Spirit of the Lord." Is this to be regarded as the same as the Holy Spirit? Might it be merely God's spirit, or might it be a personification of God's working? If these are valid possibilities, are we justified in using the Old Testament texts as evidence in constructing our understanding of the Holy Spirit and thus of the Trinity? At least one New Testament reference indicates that the Spirit of God in the Old Testament is to be identified with the Holy Spirit. In Peter's speech at Pentecost he explains the coming of the Holy Spirit in the dramatic fashion evidenced by speaking in tongues. He indicates that this is the fulfillment of what Joel had prophesied: "I will pour out my Spirit" (Acts 2:17; cf. Joel 2:28, 32). Thus, we are dealing with the same person, and are justified in using the Old Testament references to God's Spirit in formulating our understanding of the third person of the Trinity.

The Three-in-Oneness of God

The two considerations together lead, by implication, to the conclusion that if both are true, then it must also be true that God is three-in-one, or triune. Is that all we have to rely on, or can we find direct statements of this conclusion, thus establishing that our inference is correct? At first glance there appears to be one text that settles the matter conclusively by stating directly the three-in-oneness of God. That is 1 John 5:7, as found in the King James Version of the Bible: "For there are three that bear record in heaven, the Father, the Word, and the Holy Ghost: and these three are one." That should settle the matter rather definitely, should it not? Unfortunately, it does not. Other, more recent translations, such as the Revised Standard Version and the New International Version, omit this verse. What, then, are we to make of it? The reason for this "deletion" is found in the science of textual criticism. We do not have the actual document John wrote with his own hand. What we do have are later copies, which themselves are copies of copies of the original. The earliest surviving manuscripts of the New Testament are actually several centuries later than the initial writing. These many manuscripts vary among themselves in minor details of readings. The discipline of textual criticism endeavors to sift through these many manuscripts and determine, as accurately as possible, the probable original reading. One principle followed is that the earlier a manuscript, the more likely it is to be accurate, all other things being equal. What has happened is that in the more than three centuries between the translation of the King James Version and these more recent versions, a large number of manuscripts have been discovered, many of them considered more reliable than those available in 1611. And the best of these do not contain 1 John 5:7. It appears that, rather than having been written by John, those words were inserted by some copyist, perhaps as a comment, and then became incorporated into some later manuscripts.

This should not be disturbing to the faith of the believer. Our faith is based on the teaching of the original texts, as the writers penned them, and our goal should therefore be to approximate as closely as possible the actual content of those original writings. While there are severe condemnations in Scripture for subtracting from its teachings, it is important to observe that the same condemnations apply to adding to them (Deut. 4:2; 12:32; Rev. 22:18). Consequently, as much as we might wish for the clear statement of the King James on this matter, we should not insist on it if it does not really belong to the text of the Scriptures. This is not to say that what that text affirms is not true, but only that it is not explicitly asserted at this point in the biblical material. Nor, in my judgment, do any other texts in Scripture make an explicit declaration of this doctrine.

Does this, then, mean that the doctrine is not biblical? No, but it does mean that if we are to consider the doctrine of the Trinity a biblical doctrine, we must seek the evidence for it in more implicit passages, passages from which the doctrine may be deduced, perhaps after an induction of a large number of such passages. In addition, the practice of some of the characters in the biblical drama may be instructive. For example, worshiping a person indicates a belief in the deity of that person. In addition, there may be some indications that a given biblical writer was working from such an assumption, even if he does not state it overtly. It is to these that we now turn.

The Old Testament. The teaching of the Old Testament on this subject may naturally be expected to be less direct than that of the New Testament. So, for example, the idea of incarnation is not really asserted in the Old Testament. What we find instead are anomalies in the Old Testament witness, which do not necessarily teach, but are consistent with, the Trinity. They may be hints at the doctrine, which lead us to that conclusion.

One of these phenomena is the presence of plurals with respect to God, where we would not expect them. The common name for God, *Elohim* in the Hebrew, is plural in form. That particular fact may not be especially significant, however. Hebrew has something called the "plural of majesty," which is plural in form but does not necessarily indicate plurality of number. It is used of important personages, such as kings. This word, then, may not necessarily designate any sort of plurality. More significant are some of the verb forms, particularly where there is a shift in number. One of the clearest of these is Genesis 1:26: "Then God said, 'Let us make man in our image, in our likeness.'" Here the initial verb, "said," is singular, but the verb "let us make" is plural, as are the possessive endings on the nouns, "our image" and "our likeness." The import appears to be that if this is the plural of majesty, God uses it with respect to himself, but the writer does not use it of God. That this was not simply to be regarded as the plural of majesty is seen from the fact that Jewish commentators, who of course were thoroughly familiar with the language, found it necessary to offer some explanation of this plural. Some, such as the Book of Jubilees, written in the last half of the second century B.C., simply alter the reading. Philo, on the other hand, contended that God was here addressing his subordinates or inferiors, whom he utilized in the process of creation.[9] The Jerusalem Talmud, which represents first-century Judaism, argued that since 1:27 refers to one God, 1:26 must also.[10]

Another passage, which does not seem to fit into the plural of majesty explanation, is Genesis 3:22: "The man has now become like one of us." The Book of Jubilees does not have a verse corresponding to this one. The problem has been solved by omission, but that it needed to be omitted is significant. Pappias, a late-first-century Palestinian rabbi, said that the verse implied that Adam had become like an angel.[11] The earliest of the Targums, Onkelos, says "And the Lord God said, 'Behold, man is become singular in the world by himself,'" a considerable alteration of the original wording of the passage. The Palestinian Targum and the Jerusalem Targum handle the problem by asserting that God was addressing angels.[12]

Another interesting passage is Genesis 11:7, where the Lord says, "Come, let us go down and confuse their language so they will not understand each other." Philo's explanation was that God is surrounded by potencies, and when he said this, he was addressing those potencies. It was these powers who carried out the confusing of the languages, which God could not do himself, since that is an evil.[13]

In the account of the encounter between Abraham and the three men in Genesis 18 we find special considerations. There is a series of alternations between the singular and the plural. The statement about the Lord appearing to Abraham (v. 1) is in the singular, but in verse 2 Abraham sees three men. In verse 3 he addresses the visitors in the singular, "my Lord," but in verse 4, speaks to them in the plural. This alternation continues. "The Lord" is used in verses 10, 13, 14, 17, 19, and 22, but "the men" is the reference in verses 16 and 22. Then in chapter 19, two men appear to Lot, who addresses them as "Lord." These phenomena evoked a variety of responses from commentators. The Palestinian Targum maintained that three angels were sent at once rather than merely one because each carried out a different mission. No explanation is given of the fact that Abraham addressed them as "my Lord." In verse 10, the explanation is that only one angel was speaking to Abraham, and in verse 20 the Targum makes clear that "the Lord" is not to be identified with the three men, indicating rather that the Lord was speaking to the ministering angels. Philo, however, gave quite a different explanation. He maintained that there was really only one object, God, but that just as an object may cast two shadows simultaneously, God may have a threefold appearance, which he did here.[14]

One more Old Testament passage, which has received less attention than those in Genesis, is Isaiah 6:8: "Then I heard the voice of the Lord saying, 'Whom shall I send? And who will go for us?'" The shift of number from singular to plural is significant. The Targum here removes the difficulty by simply removing the plural pronoun, so that the passage reads: "Whom shall I send to prophesy, and who will go to preach?"[15]

An additional consideration from the Old Testament concerns the nature of the unity of God. The best known of the passages declaring that God is one is the Shema of Deuteronomy 6:4–5: "Hear, O Israel: The LORD our God, the LORD is one. Love the LORD your God with all your heart and with all your soul and with all your strength." The argument here is that because there is only one who is God, there should be, and need be, no dividing of the people's loyalty. The nature of that unity is important, however. There is a Hebrew word for one, *yahid,* which means simply uniqueness. It is the word used of Isaac in Jehovah's command to Abraham to offer Isaac as a sacrifice (Gen. 22:2, 12, 16). The word here, *ehad,* however, while it may also bear the meaning of the only one, can be used to speak of a unity that is actually a union or composite of several factors. It is used, for example, in Genesis 2:24: "a man will leave his father and mother and be united to his wife, and they will become one flesh." This use of this word fits well with the idea that this one is actually a union of three.

The Baptismal Formula. In the New Testament, while still implicit, the relevant data are more direct in nature. A variety of types of material is relevant to our consideration. One of the most important is the baptismal formula in Matthew 28:19, which links the three persons in such an intimate fashion as to imply equality: "Therefore go and make disciples of all nations, baptizing them in the name of the Father and of the Son and of the Holy Spirit." Coming from Jesus himself and given as the formula to be used in the administration of the important rite of baptism, this is a weighty fact. It is especially notable that while three persons are designated here, the word "name" is in the singular. There is an apparent conflict with the baptism into the name of Jesus, in Acts 8:16. The most likely explanation of this reference, however, is that this was not a prescribed formula, but simply a statement of the nature of the baptism.

Triadic References: Pauline Material. There are numerous places in Paul's writing where the three persons are grouped together. In 2 Thessalonians 2:13, 14, Paul tells the Thessalonians that God chose them to be saved, and that this was accomplished through the sanctifying work of the Holy Spirit, so that they might share the glory of Jesus Christ. In 1 Corinthians 12:4–6, Paul is speaking against the party spirit in the church at Corinth. After reminding his readers of the unity that the Spirit brings about, he relates this successively to each member of the Godhead: "There are different kinds of gifts, but the same Spirit. There are different kinds of service, but the same Lord. There are different kinds of working, but the same God works all of them in all men."

One of the most significant of Paul's references, ranking in importance with the baptismal formula, is the triadic benediction in 2 Corinthians 13:14: "May the grace of the Lord Jesus Christ, and the love of God, and the fellowship of the Holy Spirit be with you all." The close association of the three persons in this combined or at least coordinated working suggests equal status. Paul presents all of these as if they had the right to confer such blessings.

In other references of this type the association of the three persons is more subtle. In Galatians 3:11–14, Paul discusses justification, and says that a person is justified before God (the Father) by the redemptive work of Christ, so that she or he receives the promise of the Spirit. In Galatians 4:6, he says that God sent the Spirit of his Son into our hearts, who calls out, "*Abba,* Father." All three are involved in this relationship of the believer to God. Similarly, in 2 Corinthians 1:21–22, he says, "Now it is God who makes both us and you stand firm in Christ. He anointed us, set his seal of ownership on us, and put his Spirit in our hearts as a deposit, guaranteeing what is to come." Again, all three persons are part of this salvation.

In Romans 14:17–18, Paul says that the kingdom of God is not a matter of eating and drinking, but of righteousness, peace, and joy in the Holy Spirit. The reason is that anyone who serves Christ in this way is pleasing to God and approved by humans. We please God by serving Christ, which we do in the Holy Spirit. It appears from this passage that relationships to the members of the Godhead are not separable. If indeed they are a triunity, then it is not possible to relate to any of them independently. In the next chapter, Paul discusses his ministry in this triadic fashion. He speaks of the grace God gave him "to be a minister of Christ Jesus to the Gentiles with the priestly duty of proclaiming the gospel of God, so that the Gentiles might become an offering acceptable to God, sanctified by the Holy Spirit. Therefore I glory in Christ Jesus in my service to God" (vv. 16–17). He is a minister of Christ, proclaiming the gospel of God, but the aim is that the Gentiles might become acceptable to God, sanctified by the Holy Spirit. Further, he goes on to speak of what Christ has accomplished through him by the power of the Spirit (vv. 18–19). In verse 30, he urges his readers, by the Lord Jesus Christ and the love of the Spirit, to pray to God for him. His entire ministry was conducted in the context of the Triune God.

There are other triadic references in Paul's shorter letters. In
Philippians 3:3, he writes of those who worship by the Spirit of
God, who glory in Christ Jesus. In Colossians 1:3–8, he thanks
God for his readers' faith in Jesus Christ, and for their love, which
is in the Spirit. Although Ephesians is a relatively short book, it
is rich in these triadic references. Paul speaks of how the believers have been reconciled by Christ (2:13) to God the Father
(v. 16), to whom they now have access by the one Spirit (v. 18).
Ephesians 3:14–16 constitutes a prayer and a benediction for
the Ephesians. Paul kneels before the Father (v. 14) and prays
that he may strengthen the believers (v. 16), that they may be
filled with the fullness of God (v. 19), that there might be glory
to the Father in the church and in Christ Jesus (v. 21). His prayer
is that Christ may dwell in their hearts through faith (v. 17) and
that they may grasp the love of Christ (v. 18). God's strengthen-
ing of them in their inner being is through his Spirit (v. 16).

Triadic References: Other New Testament Authors. Paul is not the
only New Testament author who uses this triadic pattern. In
1 Peter 1:2, Peter addresses his readers as having been "chosen
according to the foreknowledge of God the Father, through the
sanctifying work of the Spirit, for obedience to Jesus Christ and
sprinkling by his blood." In 1 Peter 4:14, he speaks of the suffering his readers are to experience: "If you are insulted because
of the name of Christ, you are blessed, for the Spirit of glory
and of God rests on you." Addressing a similar situation of suffering, Jude urges his hearers: "build yourselves up in your most
holy faith and pray in the Holy Spirit. Keep yourselves in God's
love as you wait for the mercy of our Lord Jesus Christ to bring
you to eternal life" (vv. 20, 21).

The Book of Hebrews contains at least two references of this
triadic type. In the warning passage, 6:4–6, the author speaks
of those who have tasted the goodness of the word of God and
have been enlightened by the Holy Spirit; by falling away, they
crucify the Son of God all over again. Just as faith has a triune
reference, so also apparently does apostasy. In 10:29, although
there is no explicit mention of the Father, there is a parallel

between the Son and the Spirit: "How much more severely do you think a man deserves to be punished who has trampled the Son of God under foot, who has treated as an unholy thing the blood of the covenant that sanctified him, and who has insulted the Spirit of grace?"

One more reference deserves mention here. In Acts 20:28, Paul addresses a group of elders: "Keep watch over yourselves and all the flock of which the Holy Spirit has made you overseers. Be shepherds of the church of God, which he bought with his own blood." While there is no explicit reference to Jesus Christ, the Son, by name, it is apparent that he is the one referred to as having bought the church with his blood. If this interpretation is correct, then this is a statement of the relationship of the Triune God to the church. It is God's church, redeemed by the Son, and the Holy Spirit has appointed its overseers.

The force of these triadic references, found primarily but not exclusively in Paul's writings, is that each person of the Trinity is related to the experience of salvation, to the church and its leadership, and to the living of the Christian life, as well as to apostasy from the faith. Thus, it can be seen that for these biblical authors, to be a Christian is to be related to the Triune God, and to each of the three persons of the Trinity in terms of the unique, specific ministry of each.

The Structure of the Pauline Writings. Another, more subtle but in many ways more pervasive feature of the Pauline writings is significant in indicating that Paul thought of the Godhead in terms of a triadic pattern. When we examine the outline of his writings, it appears that Paul did not think of the working of any of the members of the Godhead without also relating this to the others. Thus, although he may be concerned primarily with one of the three, the others are successively introduced as well. This can be seen in the way several of his books unfold.

The Book of Romans, Paul's longest and most doctrinal writing, illustrates this characteristic quite clearly in its first eight chapters. From 1:18 to 3:20 Paul expounds the judgment of God on Gentiles and Jews. Then, from 3:21 to 8:1, he deals with justification through faith in Jesus Christ. Finally, 8:2–30 comprises one of the most complete biblical discussions of the Holy Spirit and life in him.

Similarly, in 1 Corinthians Paul is dealing with problems within the church, especially the issue of the unity of the church. The treatments of the different persons alternate and overlap. Initially, Paul discusses Christ as the power and wisdom of God, contrasted with the wisdom of the world (1:18–2:9). He then expounds the instruction given by the Spirit (2:10–16), after which he returns to Jesus Christ as the foundation of humans' work (3:10–15). Then comes a statement that humans are God's temple in which the Holy Spirit dwells (3:16–17). When Paul discusses the gifts of the Spirit (chaps. 12–14), he does so in the context of the welfare of the body of Christ, including the discussion of the Lord's Supper, which compares the church, as the metaphorical body of Christ, to the literal body of Christ. While simply describing, rather than analyzing, the relationship of the Son and the Spirit, against the background of the Father, it is apparent that, for Paul, they are closely connected with one another.

While Paul really does not address the Trinitarian problem in any formal fashion, at times he seems to be aware of the problem of the relationship among the three persons. This is perhaps most clearly seen in his statement in 1 Corinthians 8:6: "yet for us there is but one God, the Father, from whom all things came and for whom we live; and there is but one Lord, Jesus Christ, through whom all things came and through whom we live." While Paul does not elaborate on the statement, and the respective meanings of God and Lord are not completely clear, it appears that the uniqueness and distinction of the two persons and also the close connection of the two were within the purview of his thinking.

In Galatians, Paul was strongly concerned about the issue of justification. After defending his authority as an apostle and insisting on the necessity of the gospel message, he supports this by demonstrating the uniqueness of justification by faith in

Christ's atoning work (3:1–22). This is followed by a discussion of the status of believers as children of God (3:23–4:31). He then returns to the freedom achieved by Christ's work (5:1–15), before concluding with a discussion of the life in the Spirit, contrasting the fruit of the Spirit with the works of the flesh (5:16–6:10).

In all these books, the triadic pattern of Father, Son, and Holy Spirit is clearly present, although the order of the three varies. Paul does not really attempt to work out the relationships among the three. While he does not indicate the relative priority of the three persons, there is a subordinationist tone to some of his passages. For example, in 1 Corinthians 15:24, he writes of Christ handing over the kingdom to the Father. In Philippians 2:1–11, he speaks of the Son's self-humiliation, how he emptied himself of the prerogatives of equality with the Father, and then was exalted by God and was given the highest name. He discusses the work of the Spirit in Romans 8:9–11 in such a way as not to distinguish sharply between the indwelling of the Holy Spirit and of the Son.

John deals more directly than any other New Testament writer with the relationship of the members of the Trinity. One of the best known of such passages is the prologue to his Gospel. Here he says, "The Word was with God, and the Word was God" (1:1). While there has been considerable debate over the meaning of the first "God" without the article, it appears that John is in some sense affirming the deity of the Son and yet distinguishing the Son from the Father.[16]

Of special importance are John's statements reporting Jesus' sayings about the equivalence of relationship or action of the Son and the Father. For example, in John 14:23, "Jesus replied, 'If anyone loves me, he will obey my teaching. My Father will love him, and we will come to him and make our home with him. He who does not love me will not obey my teaching. These words you hear are not my own; they belong to the Father who sent me.'" Here obedience to Jesus' words brings a relationship to the Father; the words are not merely those of the Son, however, but belong to the Father as well. To be related to the one is to be related to the other, but Father and Son are not simply different names for the same person. They are closely related and their actions are intertwined.

A similar passage is John 14:20–21. After informing his listeners that "I am in my Father, and you are in me, and I am in you," Jesus goes on to say, "Whoever has my commands and obeys them, he is the one who loves me. He who loves me will be loved by my Father, and I too will love him and show myself to him." Because he is in the Father, the person keeping his commands is apparently also keeping the Father's commands and is loved by the Father.

In chapter 5, John gives several indications of ways in which being related to him affects the relationship to the Father. Whoever hears Jesus' words and does them has eternal life and is not condemned (v. 24). In the future, the dead will hear the voice of the Son of God and will live (v. 25) because the Father has granted the Son authority to judge (vv. 26–27). Those he is speaking to do not have the Father's word dwelling in them, because they do not believe the one he sent (v. 38). Doing the works God requires involves believing in the one he has sent (v. 29). Similarly, in chapter 8, Jesus answers the question, "Where is your father?" by saying, "You do not know me or my Father. If you knew me, you would know my Father also" (v. 19). Later in the chapter he says, "If God were your Father, you would love me, for I came from God and now am here. I have not come on my own; but he sent me" (v. 42).

In John 12:44–45, Jesus says explicitly, "When a man believes in me, he does not believe in me only, but in the one who sent me. When he looks at me, he sees the one who sent me." Similarly, in John 14:7, Jesus is reported as saying, "If you really knew me, you would know my Father as well. From now on, you do know him and have seen him," and the idea is repeated in verse 9. The converse also appears, in 15:23–24: "He who hates me hates my Father as well. . . . But now they have seen these miracles, and yet they hated both me and my Father."

Later, he says of those who will kill his followers: "They will do such things because they have not known the Father or me" (16:3).

John's epistles also contain parallels to these teachings. In 1 John 2:24, John writes, "See that what you have heard from the beginning remains in you. If it does, you also will remain in the Son and in the Father." In 1 John 4:12–16, he indicates that being in God depends on acknowledging the Son whom he has sent, and we know we have this relationship because of the Spirit God has sent.

In addition to these numerous passages declaring that relationship to the Father and relationship to the Son are connected, there is a group of passages that emphasize the unity of the Father and the Son. In John 10:28, 29, Jesus speaks of his followers' security: "I give them eternal life, and they shall never perish; no one can snatch them out of my hand. My Father, who has given them to me, is greater than all; no one can snatch them out of my Father's hand. I and the Father are one." In his prayer in John 17:11–23, Jesus prays for the unity of the believers, and twice explicitly relates this to his unity with the Father: "that they may be one as we are one" (vv. 11, 22). In verse 21 he says, "that all of them may be one, Father, just as you are in me and I am in you." In verse 23 he prays, "May they be brought to complete unity to let the world know that you sent me and have loved them even as you have loved me." Receiving glory from the Son is indirectly also receiving it from the Father (v. 22). Jesus adds, "I in them and you in me" (v. 23). The idea of the Father being in the Son and the Son in the Father is also found in John 10:38. In John 13:31, the glorification of the Father and the Son seem virtually inseparable. Then in chapter 14, Philip asks to see the Father, and Jesus replies, "Don't you believe that I am in the Father, and that the Father is in me? The words I say to you are not just my own. Rather, it is the Father, living in me, who is doing his work. Believe me when I say that I am in the Father and the Father is in me; or at least believe on the evidence of the miracles themselves" (vv. 10–11).

Another interesting consideration is how John emphasizes the Sonship of Jesus and the Fatherhood of God—much more strongly than any other New Testament writer. This can be verified by simple statistical analysis. Vincent Taylor has calculated that the title "Father" occurs 121 times in John's Gospel and 16 times in his letters, compared with 123 times in the entire rest of the New Testament.[17] Almost as impressive is the fact that the word "Son" is used 28 times in John's Gospel, 24 times in his epistles, and 67 times in the remainder of the New Testament.[18]

Finally there is a group of passages that indicate very close contact with, or knowledge of, the Father by the Son. The prologue of the Gospel contains two statements of this type. Verse 14 says, "The Word became flesh and made his dwelling among us. We have seen his glory, the glory of the One and Only, who came from the Father, full of grace and truth." In verse 18 John writes, "No one has ever seen God, but God the One and Only, who is at the Father's side, has made him known." Jesus makes a similar statement in 6:46: "No one has seen the Father except the one who is from God; only he has seen the Father." In John 8, the report of Jesus' discussion with the Jews, there are three references of this general type. In verse 42, Jesus claims to have come from God; in verse 55, he claims knowledge of the Father that they do not have, and in verse 58 he makes the boldest claim: "I tell you the truth, before Abraham was born, I am!" This last statement was evidently understood to be a claim to deity, for the Jews took up stones to stone him.

We may say, then, that when the whole text of Scripture is taken seriously, the doctrine of the Trinity emerges. It teaches clearly that God is one and is unique, that he is the only God that is true and exists. It teaches, either directly or indirectly, that there are three persons who are fully divine, the Father, the Son, and the Holy Spirit. And it also teaches, indirectly and by implication, that these three are one.

Does the Doctrine of the Trinity Make Sense?

W e now find ourselves in a serious dilemma. On the one hand, on the basis of what we examined in the previous chapter, we conclude that, if we hold to the authority of the Bible, we are driven to affirm something like the doctrine of the Trinity, namely, that God is one and that there are three who in Scripture are identified as being God or being of a divine nature: the Father, the Son, and the Holy Spirit. Thus, it seems we must believe that God is three in one.

On the other hand, we face the question of whether it really is possible to believe this unusual doctrine. For it seems to defy our logical understanding. How can it be that God is three and that he is one? For if he is three, then he cannot also be one, and if he is one, he cannot also be three. At best, the doctrine is puzzling; at worst, it is an outright contradiction. Thus, it appears that while on biblical grounds we must believe it, on logical or rational grounds we cannot believe it. Must we choose between our Christian commitment and our rationality?

Some of our contemporaries contend that this is not really a problem, or at least, not a significant problem. For the conception that only what is noncontradictory can be believed is held by them to be an outmoded idea, tied to the rationalism of the modern period, but now supplanted by something called post-modernism. We therefore need not resolve the apparent tension between divine threeness and divine oneness.

I would suggest, however, that this is not how people function in everyday life, no matter what culture they participate in. If I go into a supermarket, select three loaves of bread, and go through a checkout lane, the checkout person will ring up three loaves of bread. All my protestations that I have only one loaf will be of no avail. For in the ordinary world of human trans-actions, my claim that I have only one loaf and the supermar-ket employee's claim that I have three cannot both be true. Both may be false (I may have two loaves, four loaves, or no loaves), but they cannot both be true. Thus, it is the case that if we tell someone, or, for that matter, tell ourselves, that God is three and that he also is one, we will encounter difficulty in believing.

All of this has had the effect of making Christians who believe this strange doctrine seem incoherent. In fact, the charge has been made that "Christians are people who cannot add." Must we be condemned to being thought of this way, if we are to con-tinue to hold this doctrine? Must we call on Christian believers and would-be believers to engage in what is sometimes called "crucifixion of the intellect"? Some have even made this logi-cal tension a virtue. Tertullian in the third century contended that Christian faith (Jerusalem) had nothing to do with philo-sophical wisdom (Athens).[1] Kierkegaard in the nineteenth cen-tury maintained that the Christian faith is inherently paradox-ical, and thus, because it offends the rational intellect, makes genuine faith both possible and necessary.[2]

If God is infinite and we are finite, we will never be fully able to understand him. The fullness of what he is will exceed our powers to grasp. Thus, we cannot expect ever to resolve fully this great mystery. Having said that, however, is it possible that we may at least be able to alleviate the tension somewhat, to make the mystery partially understandable? In general, most attempts to explain the Trinity have fallen into two major types: those that emphasize the oneness and seek to explain the three-ness of God in light of this, and those that emphasize the three-ness and treat the oneness in relationship to it. The former tend, however, toward some type of modalism, that is, the view that God is simply one person, with three different modes of exis-tence. The latter, on the other hand, tend toward tritheism, that is, the belief in three Gods. I have observed that in practice many Christians tend to alternate between these two positions, and something of this alternation may be a practical necessity.

Before proceeding further, however, we need to ask more precisely just what is meant by a contradiction. A statement is contradictory if it affirms two contradictory things about the same subject at the same time and in the same respect. With this in mind, we may have a hint as to how an apparent contra-diction may not actually be that. If I say, "My house is white" and "My house is gray," I am not making a contradictory state-ment unless I mean that it is both gray and white at the same time and in the same respect. Perhaps I have repainted my house, which formerly was white, gray. If the statements were made a month apart, both are true, but they are not contradictory because they are not affirming that the house is gray at the same time as it is white. Or perhaps the walls of the house are gray, but the trim is white. Thus different parts of the house are gray and white. While it is gray and white at the same time, it is not both gray and white in the same respect. The doctrine of the Trinity is contradictory only if God is three at the same time as he is one and in the same respect as he is one. The effort of Christian theologians down through the years has been to dis-cern the difference in God being one and also being three. It is therefore not the same as claiming that a particular triangle has four corners.

When closely examined, we find that we really cannot believe a contradiction, because we do not know what to believe, or more specifically, which of the contradictory statements to believe. It is the difficulty with the liar's paradox. If someone says to you, "I am not now telling you the truth," or "the statement I am uttering is untrue," do you believe that statement or not? The problem is that if the statement is true, it is consequently false. If the implication is not direct within one statement, it may be easier to fail to see the contradiction, such as in the American Philosophical Association T-shirt, on the front of which appears the sentence, "The sentence on the back of this shirt is false," and on the back of which is the sentence, "The sentence on the front of this shirt is true." One can believe either of these sentences, but not both simultaneously. If there is a sufficient number of intervening statements between the two that contradict each other, it may be even less obvious, but the problem, when seen, is just as severe. Even those who deny the law of contradiction cannot avoid assuming it, for if they are claiming that their statements are in some sense true, then they cannot also be false. We cannot simply dismiss the logical problem.

Yet it will not be sufficient to state the doctrine of the Trinity in terms that do not contradict one another. We must seek to give some actual and concrete content to the doctrine, so that we know not simply what we do not believe or what we disbelieve, but what it is that we *do* believe. For some persons, it is not the case that they do not believe the Trinity. For them, it is a matter of not knowing whether they believe or disbelieve, because they do not know what the doctrine says. It is one thing to be asked to take something by faith, but something quite different to be asked to take something by faith when one does not know what he or she is being asked to believe. Unbelief may not actually be disbelief, if there is lack of understanding of the concept of the doctrine. Similarly, failure to reject a doctrine may not indicate that there really is positive belief in the doctrine. In this latter case, apparent belief may actually be a small-scale case of "belief in the great whatever."

This does not mean that complete and absolutely accurate understanding of the Trinity is essential for one to be a true Christian. We are saved by our trust in Jesus Christ and in the Triune God, not by our subscription to correct theology. Yet if, as we show in the next chapter, our spiritual lives are benefited and enriched by the doctrine of the Trinity, then the better we understand the doctrine, the stronger will be that relationship.

Historical Efforts at Explaining the Trinity

From the earliest days of the church, Christians have endeavored to give some elucidation of the Trinity. Interestingly, many of the more recent understandings of the Trinity are merely reworded versions or variations of those classical statements. Since George Santayana was correct in his famous statement that "those who cannot remember the past are condemned to repeat it,"[3] it may be beneficial to look briefly at some of those explanations and see whether they could be considered satisfactory. These are primarily questions about the nature of Jesus and his relationship to the Father. There are two reasons why attention first focused there. First, the full understanding of the Holy Spirit was not worked out as early as the understanding of the Son. Second, the logical difficulty is acute at the point of considering a second person divine. Adding a third person does not really change the difficulty of the problem appreciably.

Redefining the Deity of Christ. One view has been termed "dynamic monarchianism," because it sought to preserve, above all else, the full supremacy of God the Father and did so by emphasizing the Father's active working within the Son. This view also combined within it adoptionism. This is the teaching that Jesus was not in any sense divine from the moment of his conception or birth, but was at some point in his life elevated to a position of divinity, in some sense. Because of the strong monotheistic teaching of ancient Judaism, these Christians felt they must preserve this distinctive. Thus, these people were asking in what way they could understand the nature of Jesus. Basically, their solution was to contend that before his baptism, Jesus was simply an ordinary man, no different from anyone else. At his baptism, however, as the biblical text indicates, the Holy Spirit came on him in a remarkable fashion.[4] It was the power of God indwelling him. Thus, because God's power and activ-

ity were so strongly present in him, it is appropriate to speak of
him as one with the Father. Yet this oneness must not be thought
of as a metaphysical matter, that is, as being changed into the
very same nature as the Father. Rather, the oneness was a moral
oneness.[5] The analogy on which to think of the relationship of
the presence of the divine in Christ, according to Jaroslav Pelikan,
is that of the union of the Christian with the "inner man," or
the relationship of the Old Testament prophets to the Spirit,
who inspired them to speak and to write.[6]

This approach had the virtue of relieving the tension between
the seeming deity of the Son and that of the Father. It did this
by redefining that deity so that it was not so much that Jesus was
God, as that God was present and at work in Jesus. The perfect
text for this view was 2 Corinthians 5:19, "that God was rec-
onciling the world to himself in Christ, not counting men's sins
against them. And he has committed to us the message of reconciliation." This makes the difference between Jesus and Christians one of degree rather than of kind. It was not that God was
in Jesus in a way in which he is not in believers, but rather, to
an extent to which he is not at work in us.

Despite the apparent solution that this approach offered, the
church officially decided that it was not satisfactory, condemn-
ing it in a council made up of bishops from throughout Chris-
tendom.[7] Looking back from our vantage point in history, we
can see that they acted wisely in this ruling. For dynamic monarchianism bought that solution at far too great a price. It mus-
tered a single text in its support, a text that does not necessarily teach what they claimed it taught, but it did so by denying or
rejecting many Scripture passages that taught not only the qualitative identity of nature of Jesus with the Father, but also the
preexistence of the second person of the Trinity and the incarnation as a reality from the very point of conception.

This view is not simply something of the past. The Scottish
theologian, W. Robertson Smith, accused of denying Jesus' divinity, is alleged to have said, "How can they say that? I've never
denied the divinity of any man, let alone Jesus." And a song

which many orthodox Christians have sung for years, "Lord, We Are Able," contains an interesting line: "Our spirits are thine; Remold them, make us, like thee divine."

Denying the Distinction of the Son from the Father. A second "solution" took a rather different approach. Instead of denying or modifying the understanding of Jesus as God, this approach clearly taught that Jesus was God in the same sense and to the same degree as the Father. In fact, it maintained that the Son was the Father, and the Father was the Son. They were one identical person. It was the Father who entered the womb of Mary, was born as Jesus of Nazareth, suffered, died, and was resurrected. The distinctions of Father, Son, and Holy Spirit are not real distinctions as persons, but rather are distinct roles which the one God plays successively through different periods of history.[8]

On this model, God is like an actor who plays several different parts in a play, donning different costumes and makeup as he or she does. At one time I lived next door to an actor who did a number of programs for a Christian radio station in that city, including one nationally syndicated program. One day I asked him what he had done that day, and he told me about a program he and two others had taped. He said, "There were three of us actors, and together we played a total of eleven characters." That is the sense in which these Christians felt God Jesus was divine. His statement, "I and the Father are one" (John 10:30), is to be taken completely literally. In later versions of this view, the idea was advanced that God played the role of Father in the Old Testament, of Jesus in the Gospels, and of the Holy Spirit in the Book of Acts and the Epistles.

We have here a genuinely creative, and in some ways brilliant, solution to the problem. It allows for the three to be completely divine, and most emphatically preserves the unity of the Godhead. Further, it fits well with the obvious fact that the Father has greatest prominence in the Old Testament, as does the Son in the Gospels and the Holy Spirit in the remainder of the New Testament. It also fits well with Jesus' statement that he must go away if the Holy Spirit is to come. Yet, despite these virtues, we must also judge this solution to be unsatisfactory, as did the third-century church. For too many problems are involved when one looks at the full teaching of Scripture, especially of the Gospels. There are places where two or all three of the persons appear on the stage simultaneously, such as at the baptism of Jesus, when the Father spoke from heaven and the Spirit descended on Jesus like a dove (Luke 3:21–22). When Jesus prayed during his ministry on earth, to whom did he pray? And when God was the little infant Jesus, or a fetus in the womb of Mary, was he, in that form, controlling and preserving the universe? How could God truly become limited in knowledge and power in the incarnate Jesus, and still have the relationship to the creation that deity must have? These and other problems make this an unacceptable explanation.

Let us not think that this is a long-forgotten or obscure and esoteric view, however. During my Chicago pastorate, I led a young couple to personal faith in Jesus Christ. When their attendance at church began to be rather irregular, however, I visited them in their home. The husband explained to me that he had always had difficulty with the doctrine of the Trinity, and I acknowledged a similar difficulty myself. But, he said, a fellow-worker had shared with him the teaching of his church, and it had solved this difficult problem. He gave me a tract from that church, and I immediately recognized their teachings as precisely this modalistic doctrine that the church rejected so long ago. There are churches, very conservative and biblical in their other doctrines, who have embraced this particular teaching. Once again, a seemingly promising proposal can be seen to have paid too high a price for resolving the tension of the Trinity.

Redefining the Relationship between the Father and the Son. A final type of solution was to restate the nature of the relationship between the Father and the Son. Rather than holding that both were eternal and equal and as ultimately God as one another, this view contended the idea that the Son was a creature, brought into being by the Father. He was, to be sure, the highest of the creatures, but a creature, nonetheless. He was the intermediary between the Father and the rest of the creation, the agent through whom the Father had accomplished his work of creating. Taking Proverbs 8:22–31 as a messianic statement, these Christians concluded that it constituted evidence in support of their theory, especially verses 22–23: "The LORD brought me forth as the first of his works, before his deeds of old; I was appointed from eternity, from the beginning, before the world began." It might be appropriate to call him a god, a sort of demigod, but it certainly was not the case that he was the same sort of God as was the Father.[9] Other biblical texts which also seemed to support this doctrine of the superiority of the Father and the inferiority of the Son include the following:

> Passages in which Jesus indicates his inferiority to the Father, such as "the Father is greater than I" (John 14:28)
> Passages in which Jesus clearly distinguishes himself from God, such as "'Why do you call me good?' Jesus answered. 'No one is good—except God alone'" (Mark 10:18; Luke 18:19).
> Passages which indicate limitation of knowledge or power, such as "No one knows about that day or hour, not even the angels in heaven, nor the Son, but only the Father" (Mark 13:32).
> Passages indicating growth or development within Jesus, such as "And Jesus grew in wisdom and stature, and in favor with God and men" (Luke 2:52).

Taken individually, texts such as these may not be impressive. When looked at collectively, however, they do seem to project a picture consonant with the idea that the Son is the highest creature, a step down from God the Father.

This idea, once again, did not die with its condemnation by a church council. Rather, it lives on in our day. Recently two young women rang our doorbell. Because both my wife and I were busy, I was unable to invite them in. I knew, however, what they were and what they believed. They represent a relatively large, active, and growing group which call themselves Jehovah's Witnesses, and their view of Jesus Christ and of the Trinity is precisely that which we have just described. The ancient heresy of Arianism is alive and well.

When the Council of Nicea in 325 condemned the Arian view, that was not the end of the matter, however. The term the official statement of the Council used was *homoousious,* which means, literally, "of the same essence or nature." One party came very close to this position without actually adopting it. They, referred to as semi-Arians, maintained that Jesus was not *homoousios* with the Father, but *homoiousios,* similar in nature.[10] This seemingly slight variation was also deemed by the church to be an incomplete understanding of the nature of the Son. The historian Gibbon ridiculed this as a furious contest over the difference caused by a single diphthong.[11] Yet in the church's judgment, there is a vast difference between a Jesus who is the same as the Father and a Jesus who is merely similar to the Father. The former could bear the sins of humanity; the latter could not. As small as a single letter or a punctuation mark may be, its presence may make a vast difference in meaning. For example, one satirist a few years ago restated the title of Daniel Day Williams's book, *What Present-Day Theologians Are Thinking,* as *What! Present-Day Theologians Are Thinking?*[12] And I once produced a church bulletin that congratulated a newly married couple who had been "untied in marriage" (I replaced it before it was distributed). Small differences can have large implications.

The Orthodox Formula. Faced with theories such as these we have just examined, the church, meeting in council, decided that none of them was sufficient. Its bishops, meeting at Chalcedon in the year 451, sought to enunciate the true meaning of the Trinity by declaring that God is one nature or essence or substance but three persons. In a sense, however, this was not really the answer but the question. It indicated what the correct doctrine was not, but did not really give content to what God is. What do "substance" and "person" mean in this context? To us today, the word "person" suggests a distinct individual, but in that time, it meant something more like our word "persona," the mask worn by an actor on the stage. We will need to seek more contemporary analogies that enable us to make sense of the teaching in a world not as familiar with Greek metaphysics.

The Search for Analogies

One way of attempting to understand how God can be three and one is to seek analogies, parallel examples of ways in which something is three and yet also one. Christians have drawn these analogies or illustrations from a variety of realms, but especially from the physical universe. Most Christians are familiar with many of these. The Trinity has been likened to water, which can exist in solid, liquid, or vaporous form. The Trinity is sometimes compared to an egg, which includes the shell, yoke, and white. Sometimes it is likened to some object comprised of parts, such as a pair of scissors or a pair of pants. All of these, of course, have some defects. Either they make the persons of the Trinity seem like parts or pieces of the God-head, or they analogize the Trinity to something that is in different forms at different times or under different conditions, but not truly simultaneously.

Almost sixteen centuries ago, the theologian/philosopher Augustine wrote a major work on the Trinity. It was the product of many years of work, and represented his attempt to come to grips with this great mystery. He observed that of all the created objects, only the human was made in the image of God. This being the case, it seemed reasonable to Augustine that if God is triune, the best reflection of or analogy to his triune nature would be found in the creature that bears his image. Consequently, he searched for dimensions of human personality that would shed light on the triune nature of God.

The basic premise of Augustine's argument was sound, even though the specific form it took has some shortcomings from our standpoint today. What we are seeking are images that will utilize and do justice to some of what we now know about human personality. Here it is helpful to note the considerable cultural gap which exists between us in the twentieth and twenty-first centuries and the formulations given so many centuries ago. For one thing, the terminology used in that day did not bear precisely the exact meaning it carries for us today. Specifically, the Latin term *persona* or the Greek term *hypostasis,* while best translated as "person," did not mean exactly what we mean by the word "person" today in American English. We must be careful not to read back some twentieth- or twenty-first century ideas into the thought of the early church councils, and even into the content of Scripture. Further, those theologians were working with a philosophical vehicle that included concepts such as substance, which are not meaningful to large numbers of people today, and for many technical philosophers are not tenable in light of some things we now understand from science and other disciplines.

One approach considers the term "Son" to be the key to understanding the relationship between at least the first two members of the Trinity. Perhaps, says this view, God is triune and God is eternal, but God has not always or eternally been a Trinity. Thus, at least for a time there was no Trinity, only a unity, so for that period at least we do not face the apparent tension between the oneness and the threeness. God is to be thought of as the Father because at some point he brought the Son into existence. The analogy of Father and Son should therefore be thought of as more than just a metaphor. The full outworking of this version is generally that the begetting was more like an adoption than a birth. At some point in the life of the man Jesus of Nazareth, God, on the basis of Jesus' unusual receptivity, spirituality, and obedience, accepted him as his Son and elevated him to deity. He adopted him. The point with which this is usually identified is the baptism, where the Spirit descends upon Jesus, and the Father says, "You are my Son, whom I love" (Luke 3:22).

While this theory has the virtue of taking seriously an important biblical term, it faces difficulty in the biblical teaching of Jesus' preexistence. This is seen in a number of Jesus' statements. Most prominent of these was his claim, "I tell you the truth, before Abraham was born, I am!" (John 8:58). Preexistence is also asserted in his prayer on the eve of his betrayal: "And now, Father, glorify me in your presence with the glory I had with you before the world began" (John 17:5). It is also implied in John 6:62: "What if you see the Son of Man ascend to where he was before!" Paul also clearly asserted this doctrine in Philippians 2:6 and Colossians 1:15, and alluded to it in 1 Corinthians 8:6 and 2 Corinthians 8:9. Thus this idea must be abandoned as not preserving the full biblical picture of the second person of the Trinity.

One, which emphasizes the oneness more than the threeness, is the idea of a single human person who occupies different roles in various areas of his or her experience. Thus, a given person may be a husband and father, a church member, and an employee of a corporation. These different roles frequently interact with one another, and may even conflict. This is then thought to be like the three persons of the Trinity, who are capable of fulfilling different roles, simultaneously. The drawback of this analogy is that the distinction comes into play particularly when there is disagreement or tension between the roles. When they are in perfect harmony, there is little evidence of there being more than one. Indeed, the most dramatic examples of such differentiation of roles are found in cases of abnormal psychology. Modalistic tendencies are implied by this analogy.

Another analogy, which conveys the opposite emphasis, is the idea of identical twins. These are separate persons, yet genetically are identical to one another. Another closely related analogy, which would prove preferable to those theologians who hold that the Son is eternally begotten or generated, is that of clones. This also includes the idea of genetic identity, but with one person derived from the other. The point in both of these is that qualitatively (at least so far as the characteristics of the person are hereditary, rather than environmental), the two persons are identical. This would argue for a common essence, which fits the idea of God as three persons with one essence.

Some have offered the idea of an "influence Christology" as the solution to the problem. Donald Baillie found the key to the deity of Christ in the Pauline passage, "God was in Christ" (2 Cor. 5:19), and utilized that clause as the title of his book.[13]

On this view, it is more correct to say that God was in Christ than to say that Christ was God. The correct analogy to be used is that of God or Christ at work in the believer, to which Scripture frequently alludes (e.g., John 15; Col. 1:27). This means that God was present and active in Christ, at work in him, but not that Jesus was in any sense metaphysically divine. This gives us an ability to identify with Jesus, and in particular, enables us to recognize his full humanity. This approach suffers at two points, however.

First, it requires us to understand an obscure concept by means of another, which is also obscure. We do not fully understand how Christ dwells and works in us, and one mystery is not really explained by means of another mystery. Beyond that, however, this conflicts with some of the passages, such as Hebrews 1:3 ("The Son is the radiance of God's glory and the exact representation of his being, sustaining all things by his powerful word") and Philippians 2:6 ("being in very nature God, did not consider equality with God something to be grasped").

A somewhat similar effort illustrates the incarnation using the authorized representative of an important person, who has been given the authority to act on her or his behalf. So, on this model, Jesus was the one who acted and spoke for God, but who should not be thought of as being divine in essence. This again conflicts with the biblical witness to the real metaphysical deity of Jesus.

Sometimes the idea used is that of three persons holding the same property in joint tenancy. What belongs to the one belongs (contingently) to the other. If one party in the joint tenancy dies, the other receives that person's share. Neither can act without the other, however. To sell or give away the whole requires action on the part of both. Similarly, in a partnership, each partner becomes liable for the actions of the other. These analogies stress the threeness more than the oneness. The oneness is more of a legal or biological oneness than a oneness of essence. It appears that if the model is to convey the idea of three in some close bond with one another, a stronger analogy will need to be found.

One ancient theme which has recently been strongly revived is *perichoresis.* [14] This is the idea of the interpenetration of life and personality within the Godhead, the idea that the Father, Son, and Holy Spirit are bound together in such a close unity that the life of each flows through each of the others, and each has access to the thought and experience of others. It is seen as a very strong version of human empathy.

This understanding rests on the conception that the most basic or fundamental reality is spiritual. We do not hold to an ultimate dualism, that is, a view in which there are two ultimate principles, the spiritual and the material. "In the beginning God . . ." (Gen. 1:1) is how the creation account commences, and "God is spirit," we are told in John (4:24). Thus, spirit and personality have always been, and matter came into existence through the creative act of the supreme person, God. If this is the case, then personality is the key to understanding the mystery of the Trinity.

In this scheme, it is important to emphasize that the spiritual reality of which we are speaking is personal in nature. This may seem to be an obvious and unnecessary statement, but is needed in our day. There are numerous religious persons, predominantly in the Eastern part of the world, but also in the United States, whose understanding of reality is that it is spiritual but not personal. God, on this model, is present within everything, and is everything. This is pantheism. The deity of this religious philosophy is spiritual and universal, but he is really not a person, with whom one can interact. The ultimate reality, which existed before anything else came into being, is a person.

Personality involves the idea of interaction with other persons, however. There is a sense in which (something like Aristotle's idea of potentiality) a person is not really fully or actively personal apart from interaction with other persons. The supreme person, according to Christian theology, did not remain solitary. He acted to bring into existence reality external to himself, and not only the physical universe, but human persons as well. These persons to a large extent exist for the purpose of having a relationship with the creating and sustaining God. As the Westminster Shorter Catechism puts it, "The chief end of man is to glorify God and enjoy him for ever."

If reality is fundamentally physical, then the primary force binding it together is electromagnetic. If, however, reality is fundamentally social, then the most powerful constituting force is that which binds persons together, namely, love. We are here using "love" as the attractive force of unselfish concern for the other person.

We therefore propose thinking of the Trinity as a society, a complex of persons, who, however, are one being. While this society of persons has dimensions to its interrelationships that we do not find among humans, there are some illuminating parallels. Love is the binding relationship within the Godhead that unites each of the persons with each of the others. The statement in 1 John 4:8, 16, "God is love," is not a definition of God, nor is it merely a statement of one attribute among others. It is a very basic characterization of God. Love is such a powerful dimension of God's nature that it binds three persons so closely that they are actually one.

There is a sense in which the fact that God is love requires that he be more than one person. Love must have both a subject and an object. Thus, prior to the creation of other persons, humans, God could not have really loved, and thus would not have been truly love. If, however, there have always been multiple persons within the Trinity itself, among whom love could be mutually exercised, expressed, and experienced, then God could always have been actively loving. Genuine love requires that there be someone who can be loved, and this would necessarily be more than mere narcissism. Thus, the Father loves the Son; the Son loves the Father; the Father loves the Holy Spirit; the Holy Spirit loves the Father; the Son loves the Holy Spirit; the Holy Spirit loves the Son. Because God is three persons, rather than two, there is a dimension of openness and extension not necessarily found in a love relationship between two persons, which can sometimes be quite closed in nature.

This idea that the oneness of the persons of the Trinity is that of love may seem rather insufficient, however. With human persons, love is not complete or perfect. There are certain factors that separate human persons, even the closest of friends or lovers, which work against their oneness, by separating or isolating them from one another. These factors are not present within the relationship among members of the Trinity, however.

The first of these separating factors is our physical bodies. We are separated, and the law of physics which states that two physical objects cannot occupy the same space will always have that effect, as seen in the collision of automobiles or football players. This physical separation has the benefit of making separate human beings individually identifiable and distinguishable, which would be more difficult if they could occupy the same space. It has the disadvantage that communication between two human persons must take place through some medium. The Greeks thought that touch was the most effective of the senses, because it did not involve a medium of perception. That actually may not be completely true, but the medium is perhaps a lesser factor than in other forms of communication. With God, however, this sort of separation does not take place among the members of the Trinity.

A second factor separating human persons from one another is differing experiences. To the extent that we have not had similar experiences we have difficulty identifying with the other, and we frequently have not had the exact same experience. This affects the communication process adversely as well. We use a particular symbol, assuming that the other person understands by it the same thing that we do. Thus, we may think we agree when we do not, or that we disagree when we are actually talking about different things. We are unable to "get inside the other person's head" to experience what he or she has experienced. In the Godhead, however, this problem does not occur. If *perichoresis* is a real matter, then each of the members of the Trinity not only experiences what the others are currently experiencing, but this has always been the case, with every experience any of them has ever had.

A third separating or isolating factor with human persons is preoccupation with one's self, one's own needs and problems, which makes it difficult to focus on, understand, or empathize with other persons. To really understand the other person requires the ability to place oneself in that person's place. Because we are so caught up with our own needs and problems, we find it difficult to really focus on the other's concerns. Because God is other-oriented, and is completely secure in himself, each of the persons of the Trinity is so also, and each is able to identify fully with the experiences of each of the others. There is nothing to distract them from this.

There is, however, one major qualification on all that we have said, namely, the incarnation. Because one member of the Trinity took human nature without ceasing to be fully divine, he became a divine-human person, not merely a divine person. Certain limitations were involved in this incarnation. Taking a physical body involved having a definite physical location, and this meant separation from the Father. Apparently during this time of incarnation, the Son did not have direct access to the consciousness of the Father and of the Holy Spirit. He did not consciously know all that the Father knew, such as the time of his second coming: "No one knows about that day or hour, not even the angels in heaven, nor the Son, but only the Father" (Matt. 24:36). It was necessary for him to pray numerous times during his earthly ministry, indicating that he apparently needed to express his thoughts and feelings to the Father.

This love that characterizes the Trinity is *agapē,* unselfish love that is concerned for the welfare of the other person. This runs contrary to the present-day emphasis on loving oneself. Yet, at certain points, this narcissistic self-love seems to be true even of God. For if, after all, these three are so closely bound together as to be inseparable and thus in some sense one, is not God really loving himself in loving the other members of the Trinity? Two observations need to be made here. There is a sense in which we love ourselves in loving another who loves us. If loving the other person includes loving those things that he or she loves, then in loving the one who loves us, we also will love ourselves, but not directly or selfishly. Further, if love is concern for the ultimate welfare of another, then there are cases in which that sort of concern for the other will mean exercising such concern for oneself. A husband, for example, knowing the sorrow his loss of health or death would bring to his wife, would be concerned for his health, for that reason. And, on a larger scale, if a nation is under attack, its chief executive would need to take steps to protect his own life, because his safety would be important to the safety and welfare of the citizens of his country. To give up his place of safety to private citizens would not be the most loving thing to do. His act for his ultimate welfare would actually be an expression of concern for the ultimate welfare of the people. So, each member of the Trinity loves himself in loving the others because each of the others loves him, and because each of the others is dependent on him.

This analogy suggests an emphasis on the distinctness of the three persons' consciousness, and yet a closeness of relationship in which the life of each flows through the others, and in which each is dependent on the others for life, and for what he is. The closeness of the relationship is seen in Jesus' teachings. A rather remarkable passage is John 14:8–11:

> Philip said, "Lord, show us the Father and that will be enough for us." Jesus answered: "Don't you know me, Philip, even after I have been among you such a long time? Anyone who has seen me has seen the Father. How can you say, 'Show us the Father'? Don't you believe that I am in the Father, and that the Father is in me? The words I say to you are not just my own. Rather, it is the Father, living in me, who is doing his work. Believe me when I say that I am in the Father and the Father is in me; or at least believe on the evidence of the miracles themselves."

Notice the emphasis on the interpenetration of the Father and the Son, and the Father's working in and through the Son. Verse 20, "On that day you will realize that I am in my Father, and you are in me, and I am in you" constitutes a transitional statement to the following chapter. There Jesus gives his teaching about himself and believers as being the vine and the branches—they are to be in him in a way similar to his being in the Father (15:9–10). Although the relationship of the believer to Jesus is only a partial metaphor for the much closer relationship of the Son to the Father, there must be some point of analogical similarity. This parallel is repeated in the high priestly prayer, where Jesus prays that his followers may be one as he and the Father are one (John 17:21, 22).

We now need to explore further the nature of this oneness. It is, as we noted in the preceding chapter, more the idea of union than of simplicity or singularity. We are thinking here of a union in which the three are so closely linked with one another that the life of each flows through the others as well. Each has immediate access to the consciousness and experiences of the others. This means that each is dependent on the others for his own life and for his being deity. It would not be possible for one of the members of the Trinity to cease to be, or to separate from the Godhead, and the other two to continue in existence as God.

It has been common to speak of the Son proceeding from the Father, or being generated from the Father. The Spirit also has been understood to proceed from, or to derive his life from the Father. The Western church added the phrase and the thought, "and from the Son," which the Eastern church did not. On the model that we are expounding, however, each of the persons proceeds from or is generated by, each of the others. There is a mutual production of each of the persons by each of the others.

It may be helpful in this connection to think of the Godhead as a spiritual organism. This means that the three are so linked together and so interdependent that they cannot exist separately. We might think, in the human body, of the heart, lungs, and brain. Each is not the person, by itself. Yet, it is only because of the union of these organs (and many others) that the person is a person at all. It would not be possible for any one or two of the three to exist without the other(s). Without any one of these vital organs (or a replacement) you would not have a human, and you would not have a human heart or lungs. You would have a dead human, and a dead heart or lungs. Each supplies each of the others with its life. So, similarly, the Father, the Son, and the Holy Spirit each supplies the others with its life. None of the three could be, or could be God, without each of the other two.

An even better example would be that of conjoined twins, or as they are more popularly known, Siamese twins, which occur when a single fertilized egg fails to divide properly. These are twins who are joined in such a way that they share some organs. There is ordinarily an interconnected circulatory system, so that the vital fluids flow through the entire conjoined body. In many cases, the two persons share some vital organs, so that they can only be surgically separated by sacrificing the life of one of them, or even both of them.

A fairly recent example is the Holton twins, Katie and Eilish, who were born to parents living just outside Dublin, Ireland. They were conjoined from the shoulder to the hip, and shared one liver and one intestinal system. They had two legs, and two arms in roughly the normal place, with two additional arms protruding from the middle of their back. They had two hearts, and the remainder of the normal organs in approximately the usual fashion, although their torso was larger and heavier than usual for a single child. The parents had to make the agonizing decision whether to approve the surgery attempting to separate them. They were determined that under no conditions would they decide to sacrifice the life of one to preserve the life of the other. Finally the decision was made to proceed with the operation, which was attempted in May 1992. Eilish survived, but Katie died after a few days. An autopsy revealed that her heart was weak and underdeveloped, and that she had been relying on the action of Eilish's heart to supply her part of their body with blood. Eilish showed strong indications of missing Katie. Here was a case where not only the bodies but the lives of the two were so intertwined that one literally depended on the other for physical survival, and the latter depended very heavily on the former psychologically. Whereas the personalities of the two twins had been quite different, Mr. and Mrs. Holton testified that Eilish who had been the more serious of the two now took on some of the personality qualities of Katie, especially her playfulness, so that, in the parents' words, "It is as if a part of Katie lives on, as well."[15]

This leads us to one additional aspect of the Triune God. The concept of *perichoresis* means that not only do the three members of the Godhead interpenetrate each other and supply their life to one another, but that all three are involved in all of the works of God. Certain of these works are primarily the doing of one of these rather than the others, but all participate to some degree in what is done. Thus, while the work of redemption and specifically atonement was accomplished by the incarnate Son, the Father and the Spirit were also involved in some sense. Similarly, while sanctification is primarily the work of the Holy Spirit, the Father and the Son are also involved.

The biblical materials regarding God's work of creation substantiate this contention. In the Old Testament, as would be expected from the progressive nature of revelation, creation is simply attributed to God. In the New Testament, however, there is a more complete and differentiated picture. One of the most helpful texts is 1 Corinthians 8:6. Because he draws on Psalm 96:5, Isaiah 37:16, and Jeremiah 10:11–12, which state that God has created all that is, Paul seems to be elaborating on the meaning of those texts. He says, "yet for us there is but one God, the Father, from whom all things came and for whom we live; and there is but one Lord, Jesus Christ, through whom all things came and through whom we live." In John 1:3 we also get an indication of the role of the Son in creation: "Through him all things were made; without him was not anything made that has been made." In Hebrews 1:10, the Father is quoted as saying to the

Son, "In the beginning, O Lord, you laid the foundations of the earth, and the heavens are the work of your hands." While it is not always possible to demonstrate the equivalence of the Old Testament Spirit of God with the Holy Spirit, these texts can probably be used collectively of the Holy Spirit, whom Peter did identify with the Old Testament Spirit of God in Acts 2:28. The relevant texts—such as Genesis 1:2; Job 26:13; 33:4; Psalm 104:30; Isaiah 40:12–13—indicate an involvement and participation of the Spirit of God in the creation process.

Less clearly, but also distinctly, Scripture indicates participation of all three members of the Trinity in the work of redemption. While it was definitely only the Son who became incarnate, suffered, died, and was resurrected, the Father sent his Son, giving him as the sacrifice for our sins (John 3:16; 1 John 4:10; Rom. 3:25). This was much like Abraham being called on to sacrifice Isaac (Gen. 22:1–19). Any sensitive and loving parent experiences vicariously the suffering of his or her child. With the Father, for whom empathy and identification with the Son were much greater, there was an experiencing of that suffering and thus a participation in the sacrifice. Even the Holy Spirit was active in the redemptive work. The Spirit had come upon Jesus and empowered his ministry. His very life was lived in the power of the Spirit. So, for example, we read that "he was led by the Spirit into the desert," to be tempted (Matt. 4:1 par.). In Luke 10:21, Jesus, "full of joy through the Holy Spirit," praised the Father. We may infer that it was by the Spirit within him that Jesus was able to offer his life as a sacrifice.

One special logical problem connected with the doctrine of the Trinity is the question of how their works are related. Certain works seem to be attributed not simply to one, but to two or all three persons of the Trinity. Probably the most prominent of these is the work of creation. This is generally attributed to the Father. In the Old Testament, it was simply the work of God. There are in the New Testament, however, indications of the work of each of the three. A prime example is Paul's statement in 1 Corinthians 8:6, where he urges his readers not to engage

in the practice of eating food offered to idols. In contrasting
God with idols, Paul follows the argument of several Old Testament passages—Psalm 96:5; Isaiah 37:16; Jeremiah 10:11–12.
The thrust is that the true God has created all that is, whereas
these false gods, these idols, are incapable of creating anything.
Paul goes on to say, "Yet for us there is one God, the Father from
whom are all things and for whom we exist, and one Lord, Jesus
Christ, through whom are all things and through whom we
exist." Here is a statement that seems to indicate dependence
of the entire creation on both the Father and the Son. This is
not the only place where creative work is attributed to the Son.
John wrote, "Through him all things were made; without him
nothing was made that has been made" (John 1:3). In Colossians 1:16 Paul says, "For by him all things were created: things
in heaven and on earth, visible and invisible, whether thrones
or powers or rulers or authorities; all things were created by
him and for him." A similar statement is Hebrews 1:10. There
are also passages which seem to indicate participation of the
Holy Spirit in the work of creation, among them Genesis 1:2;
Job 26:13; 33:4; Psalm 104:30; and Isaiah 40:12–13. The logical problem is how the Son or the Holy Spirit can be the one
who creates, if that is done by the Father.

Here it may be helpful to think of creation on the analogy of
a building that is constructed. Who is the cause of that construction? Several answers could be given, each of which would
be true in its own way. It might be said that the architect is the
cause, since he is the source of the design that is brought into
reality. This is seen, for example, in referring to a structure as
"a Frank Lloyd Wright building." The contractor evidently is
the cause, and may erect a sign proclaiming that this is "a Smith
house." Yet the people who actually build the house are the
building trades workers, the carpenters, plumbers, electricians,
and others, who actually carry out the work of construction.
The building materials suppliers, who deliver the requisite materials to the site, might be identified as the cause, for without
them, builders would be unable to build anything. One could

also say, however, that the lending agency is the cause of the building, since it supplies the necessary funds to pay all of the preceding persons. In the final analysis, however, the owners, who sign the papers authorizing all of the actual materials and labor and obligating themselves to repay the mortgage, might correctly claim to have built the house. Actually, of course, all of these build or cause the house, but each in a different way. So, it is possible to think of the Father as the originator or source of the creation, the Son as the designer or organizer of the creation, and the Spirit as the executor of the act of creation, the one who actually carries it out.

What we have attempted to do in this chapter is to offer a model or analogy of the relationships among the members of the Godhead that may better enable us to understand the Trinity. The model we have proposed emphasizes that the three persons constitute three centers of consciousness within the one being, capable of interacting with one another. We further proposed that they are, however, bound together so closely by the centripetal power of love that they are inseparable. The life of each flows through each of the others, so that each can be said to be the basis of the life of each of the others. None could exist independently of the others. Because this common divine life flows through each of the three, each experiences the consciousness of the other, and none of the works of any of them is done independently of the others. Thus, all the divine works, whether creation, redemption, sanctification, or any other, while in each case more particularly the work of one member than the others, are nonetheless the work of the entire Trinity.

In the final analysis, we have not totally resolved the logical problems of thinking of God as both three and one, but we have reduced the tension somewhat. Short of the life beyond, we will never eliminate that tension entirely. Yet it may be helpful to realize that it is not only theology that must work with some tensions in its conceptual system. Physicists encounter a similar problem in their endeavor to understand the nature of light. On the one hand, certain of its characteristics can be accounted for only by thinking of light as waves. Other characteristics of light, however, require us to conceive of it as particles of energy. It cannot, logically, be both. Physicists, however, find it necessary to consider it both. As a physics major once remarked to me, "On Monday, Wednesday, and Friday, we think of light as waves. On Tuesday, Thursday, and Saturday, we picture it as particles of energy." (Presumably physicists do not think about the nature of light on Sunday.) Similarly, as Christians we will have to live with some unresolved tension in our understanding of the Trinity, while nonetheless not falling into outright contradiction.

Does the Doctrine of the Trinity Make Any Difference?

One additional question needs to be asked. We have examined the biblical materials and concluded that the doctrine of the Trinity is indeed found there, not taught explicitly, but implicitly. We have also examined the question of whether the doctrine of the Trinity makes any sense, and answered that in the affirmative. We observed that although the doctrine that God is three and God is one seems on the surface to be a logical contradiction, it is not actually so. There are ways to think of God that, while not removing the logical problems entirely, at least enable us to see somewhat more fully how it can be that God is one in a different sense than he is three.

The remaining question is also important, however. Even if we are convinced that the doctrine of the Trinity is true, or at least, could be true, what difference would that make? Does it in any sense affect the way we conduct our lives? In other words, is it relevant?

We may immediately note two objections that have been raised to the idea of the practical significance of the doctrine.

One was posited by the philosopher Immanuel Kant. His objection was on the basis of principle, the idea that a doctrine like this could not make any difference in practice. He said, "From the doctrine of the Trinity, taken literally, nothing whatsoever can be gained for practical purposes, even if one believes that one comprehended it—and less still if one is conscious that it surpasses all our concepts."[1] It makes no difference, said Kant, whether we worship three gods or ten, because "it is impossible to extract from this difference any different rules for practical living." The other is from the twentieth-century Catholic theologian, Karl Rahner. He says that in their practical lives, Christians are almost mere "monotheists." He says, "We must be willing to admit that, should the doctrine of the Trinity have to be dropped as false, the major part of religious literature could well remain virtually unchanged."[2] Some will surely object that the incarnation is at the very heart of the Christian faith, both religiously and theologically, so that through it the Trinity is also crucially important. This, however, according to Rahner, is also irrelevant, for in actual practice the belief of these persons is that "God" became man and that "one" of the divine persons took on flesh, rather than specifically that the Logos became incarnate. He comments, "One has the feeling that, for the catechism of head and heart (as contrasted with the printed catechism), the Christian's idea of the incarnation would not have to change at all if there were no Trinity."[3] This is an empirical argument. It is not that the doctrine cannot have any practical effect, but that in actuality, it does not. How should we respond to these contentions?

We may note, in a preliminary fashion, that to some extent Rahner's assertion is correct, but that this is not necessarily determinative. It may be more a comment on the quality of the spiritual life of Christians than it is on the nature of the doctrine. Most Christians have what I term "official theology" and "unofficial theology." The former is what one formally subscribes to, the doctrines that theoretically one claims to believe. The other is the doctrines presupposed by, and revealed by, the way we actually live. These may be quite different. The discrepancy between the two may result from not thinking through our actions sufficiently, or not paying enough attention to our beliefs. What is needed is some corrective action to bring our beliefs to bear more fully on our behavior.

Part of the problem is the standpoint from which we ask the question of relevance. Much popular Christianity in the United States is strongly influenced by pragmatism, the concept that the measure of the truth of anything, including any idea of system of ideas, is how well it works. This, however, has two problematic dimensions. The first difficulty is that this is powerfully egocentric, whether on an individual or a group basis. The question is often put in terms of what Christianity can do for me as a person, as I am. It assumes, of course, that I am the best judge of what is ultimately good for me. If a particular doctrine does not "do anything" for me, forwarding my goals and fulfilling my desires, it is to be discarded.

The word "relevant," however, is not an absolute term. It is relative. It is not a matter of whether something is relevant per se, but to a particular person, or in a particular situation, or for a particular reason. At the very beginning of my teaching career I taught undergraduates, at a time when they used "relevant" and "irrelevant" in a rather careless way, without qualification or elaboration. The expressions were used emotively, almost reflexively. I found myself adopting the expression "as irrelevant as the anatomy of a penguin." Once, however, I used the expression in the meeting of a committee which included a biology professor, who tactfully pointed out that the anatomy of penguin is very relevant—to a penguin. It was a powerful reminder that relevance must always be specified with respect to particular considerations.

Suppose, for example, that I have a small, quarter-inch artist's paint brush. Is it relevant to the painting of a door? For the most part, I would have to say no, it is not very useful. While it could be used to paint the large surfaces of the door, doing so would take a very long time. A larger brush or a paint roller would be much more suitable. However, if the door contains glass inserts, with moldings around them, then the small brush may be exactly what is needed for painting those moldings. It is, in other words, very relevant to that part of the task.

Part of the problem with measuring the relevancy of something is that this is frequently conceived of in too short a time span. Some matters that make no useful difference over a short span do in the long range. For example, in skydiving, a parachute is irrelevant for much of the duration of the fall. In fact, it not only is not helpful, it is something of a disadvantage. It impedes the skydiver's fall. In the very last part of the jump, however, it is highly relevant—to the jumper's very survival. We are dealing, when measuring spiritual matters, with the ultimate in long-range considerations, for Christianity deals with matters of eternity.

In a sense, the question is not whether this doctrine of the Trinity is relevant to me; it is whether I am relevant to it and to God. If God truly is almighty, then his purposes in the world will be accomplished, and it is I who must decide whether I want to be part of that. And since God is a Triune God, part of what I must decide to align myself with is his character. If, however, I decide not to, it is not God who will be the loser, but I. The question is not, What does this doctrine do for me as I am? but rather, How should I be, and how should I conduct myself, in light of this doctrine?

The question of the relevance of this doctrine is, however, part of the larger question of whether doctrinal distinctions in general are important, or are helpful and desirable. There is a rather strong movement within Christian circles currently that would say no. Doctrine divides people who should otherwise be in fellowship and working in cooperation with one another. It keeps people out of our fellowship, who otherwise would and should be within it. It is therefore best to deemphasize such questions. If we can get people to make a commitment to Jesus Christ, if we can show how he meets their needs, and if we can get them to live and behave in certain ways, that is more important than doctrinal hairsplitting.

The problem with putting the question this way is that it really does not discriminate among different kinds of doctrinal issues. It does not ask how important these may be. Nor does it ask what type of agreement is needed for joint participation in various types of endeavors. I may be able to cooperate with an atheist in working for certain types of public policies, issues of social justice, and the like. Beyond that, however, there will be serious limitations on our ability to link arms. To go to the other extreme, it seems to make a minor (and relatively unclear) matter major, if we insist that we cannot pray together with a Christian who agrees with us on virtually all matters of doctrine, but disagrees with us on whether the church will go through the great tribulation. The question of whether God is three-in-one, however, appears to me more like the former question than like the latter. It is not minor or peripheral; it concerns the very nature of who God is.

What we are seeing today is a redefining of Christianity and of religion in general. For much of their history, Christians thought of their faith and religious life as dependent on certain truths, objects of belief. This is the meaning of the word "orthodoxy" (straight or right opinion). In the nineteenth century, however, in response to the thought of Kant, two contrasting conceptions of religion came into currency. One, following Friedrich Schleiermacher, emphasized feeling. To be religious is not to believe or think in a certain way, or to behave or act in a particular fashion. Rather, it is to feel, and especially, to feel totally dependent on God. The other approach, which in the United States culminated in the social gospel of Walter Rauschenbusch, emphasized ethical living, and especially, the endeavor to transform society. Yet both of these approaches, which sometimes blended within liberalism, have in the long run proved detrimental. Those churches and denominations which have emphasized these approaches, to the relative neglect of doctrinal beliefs, have lost their vitality and their momentum in the world.

If, then, we insist on the doctrine of the Trinity, at what points does it contribute to the spiritual well-being of Christians and churches? It does so, first, by helping alleviate some of the other intellectual problems connected with Christian belief, and some of what seem to some persons to be unethical aspects of God's nature and actions.

One of these is the problem of evil, perhaps the most serious intellectual challenge to Christian belief. The problem takes this form. If God is all-powerful, then he is able to prevent evil (natural disasters, disease, human mistreatment of other humans, etc.). If he is all-loving, he would want to prevent evil. Yet, evil is very much and very obviously part of our world.

One aspect of Christian doctrine that contributes to alleviating this problem is the incarnation. This says that God is not merely aloof or indifferent to the suffering in the world. The second person of the Trinity has acted to take some of that evil's effects on himself. Jesus suffered the consequences of all human sin, in his death on the cross. If, however, the view of the Trinity that we have been developing is correct, then it was not merely the Son who suffered those experiences. The Father and the Spirit, although not directly experiencing that suffering as their own, did experience the Son's experience of it, thus also suffering vicariously. While some may continue to fault God for allowing evil which he could have prevented, the point is that the decision to allow such evil was made with the full awareness that it would bring suffering on himself, in all of his persons. He must therefore have permitted it for the sake of a much greater good which would result.

Further, however, it removes the charge that the idea of atonement is unethical or improper. The biblical picture presents the idea that God the Son has assumed the place of humans, bearing the penalty for their sins. The Father has laid that guilt on the Son, with the consequent necessity of his death. This, however, seems to some to be a radically unethical arrangement.

The Father, rather than punishing guilty sinners, instead punishes an innocent third party. Surely this is unjust.

If, however, we have correctly understood the doctrine of the Trinity, then the three persons are not as separate from one another as we have sometimes thought and as has sometimes been alleged. The decision that one of the members of the Trinity should become incarnate, and thus should suffer the pains of being human, and beyond that, should die an atoning death for humanity, was a jointly made decision. It was not an unwilling person who was made the victim of human sin. The second person of the Trinity participated fully in the mutually made decision. He did not lose a two-to-one vote, and consequently was victimized. He chose to lay down his life. As he himself said in John 10:17–18: "The reason my Father loves me is that I lay down my life—only to take it up again. No one takes it from me, but I lay it down of my own accord. I have authority to lay it down and authority to take it up again. This command I received from my Father." Thus, the apparent injustice of an unwilling, innocent third party suffering is removed.

Sometimes a courtroom scene is employed as an illustration of the atonement. On this model, God is the judge who finds humanity guilty and passes the sentence of eternal death. Then, a third party, Jesus, steps forward and volunteers to serve the sentence in place of the convicted person. Worse yet, the picture sometimes virtually assumes that the judge selects some other innocent party, conscripts him, and punishes him instead of the perpetrator of the wrong. This model should be adjusted, however, in light of the doctrine of the Trinity as we have here developed it. The truth would be better served by seeing that the judge himself steps down from the bench, removes his robes, and proposes to serve the sentence himself. The Father, Son, and Holy Spirit are not as sharply separated as the original illustration would suggest. The Son, on behalf of the Trinity, sacrificially offers his life to the Father, who accepts it on behalf of the Trinity. There is surely nothing immoral or unethical about such an act.

Second, the doctrine of the Trinity serves to distinguish Christianity from other religions. We live in a religiously pluralistic society, at least empirically so. By that statement we mean that there are actually present within our society significant numbers of adherents of religions other than Christianity. Buddhism, Hinduism, and Islam are assuming prominent places within our society, as of course has been the case for some time with Judaism. Beyond that, however, we face the claims of ideological pluralism. By that we mean the claim either that all religions are at base the same, or that they may be different from one another but are all equally valid. They have the same outcome, that is, any of them leads to God. Actually, this latter form of pluralism reduces to the former, for it redefines what is essential in the religions so that they do not differ crucially. In one way or another, says this pluralism, the differences between Christianity and other world religions can be reconciled, or accommodated to one another.

The Trinity appears to defy this assimilation, however. For on the one hand, it distinguishes Christianity from strictly monotheistic religions, such as Judaism and Islam. On the other hand, it also distinguishes Christianity from polytheistic or pantheistic religions, including Buddhism and Hinduism. None of these contain anything quite like the doctrine of the Trinity.

Actually, there are some who would challenge this latter statement. Raimundo Panikkar, in particular, has contended that the Christian doctrine of the Trinity is simply an expression of an experience which is also found within Hinduism, and presumably in other religions as well.[4] Thus, belief in God the Father expresses an experience of God as removed, as within himself. The Son is a symbol for the experience of God as coming to us, coming forth from himself. And the Holy Spirit reflects the experience of God actually within us. Pannikar claims that these experiences are to be found within Hinduism as well.[5] This, however, makes religion primarily a matter of an experience, not belief. While space does not permit a complete discussion of this matter, such an understanding certainly appears to contradict the way Christ, the apostles, and the early church, including Paul, understood the nature of the Christianity they taught and practiced. This is, in other words, a redefinition of Christianity which seems to put it in conflict with its historical roots.

If Christianity is no different in its fundamental nature or in its effects from other world religions, then it is not crucially important that one subscribe to and follow its basic teachings. If, on the other hand, Christianity is the way to God and is distinctive from other religions, then it is important that those of such other beliefs come to subscribe to Christ's teachings and believe in him. The Trinity is what distinguishes Christianity forcefully from other religions. A powerful evangelistic and missionary implication is involved in this doctrine.

What about the practice of the Christian life, as it relates to such matters as prayer and worship? Here we are working with an assumption that prayer and worship are intimately linked. The kind of person to whom it is appropriate to direct prayer is the kind of person whom one might appropriately worship, and vice versa. We may begin by asking how the doctrine of the Trinity might affect our practice of prayer.

There are two basic views on the subject of the person to whom prayer should be directed. On the one hand, there is what I would term the "Father only" view. This says that prayer is to be addressed to the Father. Generally, this is associated with a view of the works of the Triune God that says that each work is primarily the function of one of the members of the Trinity. Thus, the Father is the creator, the Son is the redeemer, and the Holy Spirit is the sanctifier. In keeping with this scheme, the Father also does the work of providence, and consequently is the one who hears and answers prayers. Thus, we should address those prayers directly to him. This is substantiated by the fact that Jesus himself prayed to the Father, and in the sample prayer which he gave, generally referred to as "the Lord's Prayer," he instructed his followers to pray, "Our Father, who is in heaven." Note, says this view, that we find no command in Scripture to pray to any other member of the Trinity. Nor do we find such a practice.

The other approach, the "all three" theory, suggests that hearing and answering prayer is the responsibility of the Trinity. Certain works of the Trinity are primarily the work of one member, but all participate in all of the works nonetheless. Thus, while all prayers are directed to the Trinity as a whole, certain of these should especially be prayed to one member or another, as appropriate to that work. It is appropriate to ask the Father to provide for one's needs, to thank the Son for his work of redemption, and to address to the Holy Spirit the expression of desire to be more fully conformed to the likeness of Christ. Those who hold this view and engage in these practices believe they can find precedent and thus authorization for such activity in the Bible and the history of the church.

It should be apparent by now that our view of the internal relations of the Trinity would favor the second theory. While certain works are particularly the work of one member of the Trinity more than another, the *perichoresis* of the three persons is so close that each has access to the life of the others. We relate to the whole Godhead through one or the other of the members of the Trinity. Therefore, the person to whom one prays should be that person who has primary responsibility for the subject matter of the prayer.

Is there biblical support for this view, however? To be sure, there is no instance of prayer to Jesus being commanded, nor for that matter, is there such a command regarding prayer to the Holy Spirit. We do, however, find several instances of prayer to Jesus in the New Testament. One of these is Stephen's prayer, in Acts 7. He saw Jesus, standing at the right hand of the Father. As he was being stoned, he cried out, "Lord Jesus, receive my spirit" (v. 59), and "Lord, do not hold this sin against them" (v. 60). Clearly, this was a prayer directed to Jesus. Another instance is found in Paul's thorn in the flesh passage, 2 Corinthians 12. Three times he pleaded with the Lord that it might be taken away from him (v. 8). The reply was, "My grace is sufficient for you, for my power is made perfect in weakness." Paul's comment on this reply is, "Therefore I will boast all the more gladly about my weaknesses, so that Christ's power may rest on me" (v. 9). It is apparent from the linkage of "power" in the latter half of the verse with the usage of it in the first half, that it was to Christ that this prayer was directed. Here, then, is another prayer to the second person of the Trinity. One other such prayer is the "Come, Lord Jesus" in Revelation 22:20. Although uttered virtually as a formula, this is certainly a prayer, and it is directed to Jesus.

Beyond this, however, one must ask about the logical status of the believer today, as compared with that of the disciples during the time of Jesus' earthly life and ministry. The latter addressed to Jesus their expressions of praise and thanks, their requests for guidance and help, and so on. They did so directly. Presumably such expressions and requests are also appropriate and even commanded for followers of Jesus today. For such persons, however, Jesus is not bodily present, but prayer would seem to be the corresponding form that these communications would take. Thus, to argue that the disciples did not, during Jesus' time on earth, pray to him but only to the Father, seems strictly correct, but actually incorrect. They did, in his presence, what prayer would be in his absence.

What about prayer to and worship of the Holy Spirit? Here we may note that we have relatively little biblical material to draw on. Indeed, there is relatively little biblical material about the nature and work of the Holy Spirit, compared with the treatment of the Father and the Son. This may be in part because the era of special prominence of the Holy Spirit's working was yet in the future. In addition, it appears that the Holy Spirit, the inspirer of the biblical writers and thus of the writings, called attention primarily to the Father and the Son, not to himself.

One passage that has sometimes been thought to indicate worship of the Holy Spirit is Philippians 3:3: "For it is we who are the circumcision, we who worship by the Spirit of God, who glory in Christ Jesus, and who put no confidence in the flesh."

The part of the verse that is especially significant to us is the second of the "who" clauses, which in Greek reads, *oi pneumati Theou latreuontes*. The ambiguity centers on *pneumati,* which can be translated either, "the Spirit" or "in [or by] the Spirit." If the former, then this is a declaration that they worship the Spirit; if the latter translation, not so. The noun is in the dative, locative, or instrumental case, which would ordinarily favor the second translation. However, the verb *latreuō* takes the dative case, so *pneumati* would be in the dative even if it were the direct object of the verb. The correct interpretation cannot be determined on purely lexical grounds.

The next consideration regarding the correct rendering is the syntactical issue. Here the question is to what the clause "worship [by] the Spirit" is parallel. If it is a parallel to "glory in Christ Jesus," then "worship the Spirit" would be the preferred rendering. If, however, it is to be understood as parallel to "have no confidence in the flesh," that would favor the translation "worship by the Spirit." There is a neat symmetry between the clauses, "who worship the Spirit" and "glory in Christ Jesus," but "glory in Christ Jesus" is not exactly parallel to "worship the Spirit." Thus the syntactical considerations do not give us final resolution of the problem.

A final source of insight would be the contextual issue. Here the fact that Paul seems throughout the section to stress not having confidence in the flesh favors the idea of worshiping by the Spirit, depending on him, rather than worshiping him. This is not, of course, conclusive, but it renders the translation "who worship the Spirit" sufficiently unlikely that we cannot really rest such a significant practice on it.

One other passage that has sometimes been thought to relate to this issue is 1 Corinthians 6:19–20, which reads: "Do you not know that your body is a temple of the Holy Spirit, who is in you, whom you have received from God? You are not your own; you were bought at a price. Therefore honor God with your body." The idea that this verse is suggesting a worship of the Holy Spirit comes from Augustine, who translated verse 20,

"Honor the God in your body" (i.e., the Holy Spirit, who dwells within the body of the believer). The problem again revolves around the preposition *en* in verse 20. This, as we noted above, can be treated as an instrumental, "with," or a locative, "in," as well as a dative. Augustine, who did not know Greek, was working with the Latin at this point, and the Latin permits the interpretation, "the God which is in your body." The Greek, however, does not permit such a rendering, allowing only the adverbial rendering, "Glorify God in (or with) your body." Thus, this text does not support the idea of worshiping the Holy Spirit.

It appears that we cannot support the idea of worshiping or praying to the Holy Spirit from any direct statements of the New Testament, either didactic or narrative. Geoffrey Wainwright says, "So we may conclude that there is no case in which the Spirit figures as an object of worship in the New Testament writings."[6] Arthur Wainwright puts it equally strongly: "There is no evidence in the New Testament that the Spirit was worshipped or received prayer."[7] It appears, then, that in the New Testament the Holy Spirit was not the recipient, but the instrument, the enabler, of prayer. Prayer was done "in the Spirit," or "by the Spirit" rather than "to the Spirit."

If we are to find support for the practice of praying to or worshiping the Holy Spirit, we must look beyond the New Testament. The question of when this practice began is a subject of some dispute. Leonard Hodgson has affirmed that there was no early practice of this: "Now it is true, so far as I know, there is extant no instance of hymns or prayers addressed to the Holy Spirit that is certainly earlier than the tenth century. It is also true that the standard form of Christian worship is worship offered by the Christian to the Father in union with the Son through the Spirit."[8] This appears to be something of an overstatement, however. While relatively rare in the first five centuries, there are indications of worship of the Holy Spirit in conjunction with the Father and the Son, with a gradual growth of the practice of worship of the Spirit. For example, Basil of Caesarea claims that in the third century Origen used a form of the

Gloria in which the Spirit was placed on the same level with the Father and the Son.[9] There actually is evidence of such practice earlier, in some apocryphal writings. In the *Ascension of Isaiah,* both Christ and the Holy Spirit are objects of worship. This passage (9:16) occurs in a section termed "The Vision of Isaiah," which has been dated at the latest to the end of the second century, and may have been in circulation much earlier.[10] In the third-century *Acts of Thomas* there is a series of eight invocations made to the Holy Spirit.[11] These contain definite requests, which clearly are instances of prayer. So we have record of prayer to the Holy Spirit in the third and even the second centuries. Since, however, this evidence is in books not considered part of the mainstream of Christianity of the time, it does not indicate generally accepted prayer and worship.

While the growth of such practices appears to have been slow, it seemingly was stimulated by the presence of the Arian heresy. Actually, the Council of Nicea had given only the briefest of treatments to the Holy Spirit, almost in passing, saying, "and [we believe] in the Holy Spirit." The desire to avoid the Arian heresy both in theory and in practice led to a growing emphasis on worship of the Spirit. Basil was the primary leader in this development. He introduced a doxology that was intentionally anti-Arian: "to God the Father *with* the Son, *together with* the Holy Spirit." This was supported by his book *On the Holy Spirit,* in 375. He hesitated to call the Holy Spirit "God," which the New Testament did not do, and preferred to use the term *homotimos,* "same praise," as equivalent to *homoousios,* moving from the liturgical practice to the nature of the Holy Spirit. Whether it is permissible to worship the Spirit in isolation, it surely should not be improper to worship him in connection with the Father and the Son, according to Basil. He was charged with being an innovator, but responded that it was not trinitarian orthodoxy that had made the Holy Spirit equal with the Father and the Son. It was Jesus himself who had done so by giving the trinitarian baptismal formula, in Matthew 28.[12] Athanasius had earlier made much of the formula, suggesting that if one did not accept the deity of the Holy Spirit, how could the work of baptism then have its full effect? Basil went on to contend that if baptism is into the name of the Father, the Son, and the Holy Spirit, and if the Spirit is but a creature, then one has not truly been initiated into the full Godhead.[13] Further, not only in the baptismal formula and the doxology, but in the hymn sung at the lighting of the lamps each evening there was evidence of the ancient practice, which was preserved in the words: "We praise Father, Son, and God's Holy Spirit."[14] It was at the Council of Constantinople that the Holy Spirit really came into his own for the first time. Now the Spirit was declared to be *homoousios* with the Father and with the Son.

We can summarize the evidence regarding the worship of and prayer to the Holy Spirit in the following fashion. There is no evidence in the New Testament, either in instructions or in practice, of worship and prayer directed to the Holy Spirit. There is, however, considerable indication of a growing practice, as early as the third and fourth centuries. This became more firmly established as time went on.

A further consideration, however, relates to inferences that may be drawn from the doctrine of the Holy Spirit. Is what we believe about his nature such as to lead us to conclude that we should worship and pray to the Holy Spirit? Would this be appropriate, in light of who and what he is? Was the church correct in its adoption of the practice of worshiping and praying to the Spirit?

We have argued that the Holy Spirit is a person, and as such, is someone to whom human persons can relate in direct fashion. This is supported by the biblical descriptions of the personal ministry the Spirit performs in direct relationship to the individual believer. He is the one who convicts persons of sin, righteousness, and judgment (John 16:8–11); regenerates (John 3:5–8); guides into truth (John 16:13); sanctifies (Rom. 8:1–17); and empowers for service (Acts 1:8). He is the one who inspired the writers who produced the Scriptures (2 Tim.

3:16; 2 Peter 1:21). In none of these instances is it said that the Spirit works in conjunction with the Father and the Son.

Scripture also prohibits certain actions of the believer in relationship to the Holy Spirit: lying (Acts 5:3) and grieving (Eph. 4:30). These commands surely presuppose not only the possibility but the actuality of a personal relationship between the believer and the Holy Spirit, which relationship is intended to be a positive one. If, however, such relationship, whether positive or negative, is possible, what should be the nature of that interaction? To the extent that there is communication of a direct and personal nature, this communication would seem logically to be prayer. If our desire is for conviction, whether of ourselves or of others, or for a greater sanctification, or for illumination, since these are primarily the work of the Spirit, such requests should be directed in prayer to him. And, if we are truly grateful for his works, such as regeneration, it would follow that we ought to express our gratitude for that work directly to the Holy Spirit. The Holy Spirit is an appropriate recipient of our prayers, at least some of them, and what applies to prayer should also apply to worship.

It is, then, in order for the believer to pray to and worship, not just the Father, but the Triune God. Worship will be of God the Triune One, and prayer will be primarily to God the three in one. Inasmuch, however, as certain works of God in relationship to the believer are particularly the work of one or another member of the Godhead, communication with him regarding that work should be especially directed to that one person. Thus, one's prayer should be addressed to the Triune God, and at least in part, to each of the individual members of that Godhead.

The Believer's Relationships

It is now important for us to ask about the implications of the understanding of the Trinity for the believer's relationship to other humans. Here I am working with the following thesis: God has created us in his image. That image, however, is not merely structural but also dynamic and relational, and is not borne by us merely individually, but also in a collective or communitarian fashion. If this is the case, then the relationships that obtain among the members of the Trinity furnish the key to the relationships that should be present between the believer and other believers, and quite possibly, other humans regardless of their spiritual condition. We may note, however, two different views of this intra-trinitarian dynamic.

The subordinationist view says that there is an eternal, asymmetrical relationship within the Trinity between the Father and the Son, and by extension, the Spirit as well. The references to the Father begetting or generating the Son are applied, not to the incarnational status of the Son, but to all eternity. Thus, the Son derives from, and depends for his life on, the Father. There was not a point of beginning of this begetting, a time before which the Father had not brought the Son into being. From all eternity the Father has been begetting the Son, and presumably will for all time to come. The subordination of the Son to the Father was therefore not simply during his earthly life. It is from all time. Similarly, on this view the Holy Spirit proceeds from the Father, and possibly from the Son as well. This procession is not a matter merely of sending the Spirit into the world, but of his very being. Mindful of the dangers of Arianism, those who adopt this view generally take considerable pains to disclaim an inferiority of the Son to the Father.

Contrasted with this view is another, which argues for the eternal equality of the three persons of the Trinity and the symmetry of their relationships to one another in their essential status. The biblical statements about the Father begetting the Son are to be applied to the earthly incarnation, when the second person of the Trinity stepped down to earth and added humanity to his deity. Similarly, his statements of apparent subordination, such as, "the Father is greater than I" (John 14:28), are to be interpreted within this framework. This subordination is to be understood as a subordination of function, not of essence. What the three persons are is the same; they are completely equal. It is also a temporary subordination. It was for the period of Christ's earthly residence and ministry, not for all time. The same is true of the Holy Spirit, who was sent to reside within believers from the time of Pentecost until the second coming, and who therefore carries out the directives of the Father and the Son.

On this latter view, there is not an asymmetrical relationship of generation. Not only do the Son and Spirit derive their being from the Father, but they also derive it from one another, as does the Father from each of them. Beyond that, this view claims that each member of the Trinity serves each of the others. There is a mutual subordination of each to the other.

It appears to me that there is more cogency in the arguments offered in support of this latter view than those presented to justify the former view. The interpretations the orthodox gave to the passages appealed to by the Arians are basically that these should be taken as referring to Jesus' earthly ministry, rather than his eternal status. The logic of the argument would seem to apply to the passages marshaled in support of the subordinationist view as well. Thus, the begetting passages should be seen as referring to the earthly residence of Jesus, rather than some everlasting continuous generation by the Father.

Further, when some of the begetting passages are examined more closely, they present some difficulties for the former view. In Acts 13:33, for example, Paul quotes from Psalm 2: "You are my Son; today I have become your Father." Note, however, that Paul applies this to the resurrection of Jesus: "We tell you the good news: What God promised our fathers he has fulfilled for us, their children, by raising up Jesus." This does not seem to relate to some eternal begetting. The same is true of Hebrews 1:5 and 5:5, especially the latter: "So Christ also did not take upon himself the glory of becoming a high priest. But God said to him, 'You are my Son; today I have become your Father.'" This relates to the period of his earthly ministry as priest.

Further, the former view has difficulty preventing the subordination of the Son to the Father, since it is an eternal subordination, from lapsing into the inferiority of the Son, which would approximate the Arian view. Nowhere is this seen more clearly than in Geoffrey Bromiley's article in the *Baker Dictionary of Theology:* "'Generation' makes it plain that there is a divine sonship prior to the incarnation (cf. John 1:18; 1 John 4:9), that there is thus a distinction of persons within the one Godhead (John 5:26), and that between these persons there is a superiority and subordination of order (cf. John 5:19; 8:28)."[15] Bromiley adds an important qualifier to his statement, however: "Nor does his subordination imply inferiority."[16] Here a desire to avoid Arianism seems to have led to a logical absurdity. The Father is superior to the Son and the Son is subordinate to the Father, but without being inferior. It would appear that Bromiley is working with some ambiguity of superiority and inferiority that enables A to be superior to B without B being inferior to A. Without justification of this distinction of meaning we have a logical contradiction. And I would contend that if that distinction were to be made clear, the significance of the Father's superiority would vanish. In other words, if the ambiguity is not removed, there is a logical contradiction. If it is removed, the meaning of the assertion is lost.

The kenosis passage in Philippians 2 also asserts that some major change in Jesus' status took place when he became incarnate. There Paul states that being in the form of God, the one known as Christ Jesus did not think *equality* with God something to be grasped, but emptied himself and took on the form of a servant. It is apparent that a type of subordination took place in the incarnation, when Jesus stepped down from a position of equality with the Father. What, however, can be said of equality if one of the persons is dependent for his being on the other in a way in which the other is not dependent on him?

Beyond that, we should note that, especially in Paul, the three persons are not invariably named in the order, Father-Son-Spirit. Those who hold to the priority of the Father would contend that the order Father-Son-Holy Spirit is normative, indicating the superiority or priority of the Father to the Son and of both the Father and the Son to the Holy Spirit. There is, however, a lack of uniformity of this pattern in the New Testament. Indeed, occasionally the reverse order occurs, as in 1 Corinthians 12:4–6: "There are different kinds of gifts, but the same Spirit. There are different kinds of service, but the same Lord. There are different kinds of working, but the same God works all of them in all men." Another example is Ephesians 4:4–6, a passage whose content quite closely parallels the 1 Corinthians 12 passage. This may be a climactic arrangement, and thus a testimony to the order of Matthew 28:19. Yet there are passages where even the reverse order of that passage is not preserved. An instance would be the Pauline benediction in 2 Corinthians 13:14: "May the grace of the Lord Jesus Christ, and the love of God, and the fellowship of the Holy Spirit be with you all." B. B. Warfield commented on this phenomenon: "The question naturally suggests itself whether the order Father, Son, Spirit was especially significant to Paul and his fellow-writers of the New Testament. If in their conviction the very essence of the doctrine of the Trinity was embodied in this order, should we not anticipate that there should appear in their numerous allusions to the Trinity some suggestion of this conviction?"[17]

In fact, the exact names, Father, Son, and Holy Spirit, are not always used. If the fatherhood or begetting is thought to be of the very essence of the Trinity, then one would expect that these terms, Father and Son, would be used invariably. Whereas this is the case with Jesus and with John, whose wording closely approximates that of Jesus, such is not the case in Paul's writing. In fact, he appears to prefer "God" and "Lord" to "Father" and "Son." It should be noted that for Paul, raised as a strict Jew, the term "Lord" would be virtually equivalent to "God." Paul is here writing from the perspective of a worshiper, rather than a theologian, as the context would indicate. He was concerned with the relationship of the three persons to him, rather than their relationship to one another. Warfield again comments: "It remains remarkable, nevertheless, if the very essence of the Trinity were thought of by him as resident in the terms 'Father,'

'Son,' that in his numerous allusions to the Trinity in the God-head, he never betrays any sense of this."[18]

Further, we must ask about the real meaning of the terms "Father" and "Son." The assumption commonly made, and certainly present in the thinking of those who argue for the superiority of the Father, is that these terms indicate subordination and derivation of being of a Son from a Father. This is a natural assumption for us, living almost twenty centuries after the writing, and in a very different culture, for this is what Father and Son mean in our experience. This was not necessarily so in that Hebrew culture, however. Warfield claims that the word "son" for the Jews referred less to derivation from the father and more to the likeness of the son to the father. Thus, as applied to a member of the Trinity in relationship to another, it would be an indication not primarily of subordination but of equality. This can be seen from the explanation John gives of one instance of the Jews attempting to stone Jesus: "For this reason the Jews tried all the harder to kill him; not only was he breaking the Sabbath, but he was even calling God his own Father, making himself equal with God" (John 5:18).

There are other relevant passages. One is Jesus' description of the relationship that was to obtain between his disciples. The one who would be the leader must be the servant of all. He himself took the towel and basin and proceeded to wash the disciples' feet. This was a voluntary submission of oneself to equals, or in this case, to those who were, in one sense, his subordinates. It would seem to be a model based on Jesus' own action, just as Paul urged his Philippian readers to "look not only to your own interests, but to the interests of others" on the basis of Jesus' example in the incarnation.

Finally, there are indications of the mutual submission of members of the Trinity to one another, even during Jesus' earthly abode. Royce Gruenler has claimed that in the Gospel of John we find numerous instances of what he terms "mutual deference."[19] While not all of these can be regarded as establishing as clearly as he thinks the thesis he is advancing, there is material here which cannot be ignored. The Father does glorify the Son; the Son is to rule over the judgment. There are indications that outside the incarnation there is greater symmetry of the persons than the former view accredits.

We conclude, therefore, that the attribution of eternal superiority and generation to the Father and of eternal subordination and derivation to the Son is an incorrect interpretation, based on identifying too closely the economic Trinity (the Trinity as manifested to us in history) with the immanent Trinity (God as he really is in himself). Rather than one member of the Trinity being the source of the others' being, and thus superior to them, we would contend that each of the three is eternally derived from each of the others, and all three are eternally equal. Any indications of a contrary status are to be understood as referring to the temporary functional subordination of the Son to the Father, and of the Spirit to both.

If we adopt this understanding of the relationship among the persons of the Trinity, what should be the implications for our own conduct? I would suggest that, if the relationship of the members of the Trinity to one another is intended to be a model for us to follow in relating to one another, then we will be concerned to function in a relationship of equality, of mutual respect, in which we understand that others are as important to God as we are, and treat them as equals.

What would this mean? It would mean, first, that in the church all Christians and all church members will be regarded as equal in value. If indeed all Christians are indwelt by the Holy Spirit, and thus have equal access to the Spirit's guidance, then the insight and judgment of each will be valued. Just as a democracy has a "one person, one vote" principle, this should be even more powerfully operative within the church. While not intending to derive a specific form of church government from this, it should be apparent that any situation where one member dominates or coerces another is improper.

Anyone who has spent any time actively involved in a church knows that, in practice, not everyone is equal. Rather, as someone has put it, "some people are more equal than others." Not only are some people more influential, their opinions being more highly regarded than others, but some people may not be sufficiently sensitive to the opinions and feelings of others. There are people who insist on having their way, sometimes running roughshod over others. Whether expressed or not, the message conveyed seems to be, "My way or no way." In my judgment, one of the major sources of difficulty in congregational life today is the presence of highly assertive persons, who act in this way. More than one pastor has found himself blessed with a lay leader who wants to tell him what to do, and conversely, there are churches that have suffered at the hands of a pastor who acts unilaterally, to say nothing of lay persons experiencing such domination at the hands of other lay persons.

This is not to say that there are not persons who, by virtue of experience or other qualifications, or of spiritual maturity, should play more significant parts in congregational decision making. There will indeed be functional differences in such a group, and there must be. A football team without a quarterback who calls the plays would not be very successful. We are rather concerned with the idea that every person is significant, and should neither be ignored nor coerced. In the final analysis, majority must be followed, but the way in which the minority is treated will reflect our understanding of the dynamic within the body of Christ.

This means as well that each person is important within the body, whether he or she occupies a more or less conspicuous role within it. There are, to be sure, some persons whose talents are greater and whose public contribution is more evident than that of others. Perhaps they are even heavy givers to the work of the church. There is a natural human tendency to value such persons more highly than we do others, of more modest gifts and station. This is not how it should be, however, and not how it is in the sight of God. Two passages come immediately to mind. One was Jesus' comment on the widow who gave the two small coins, as contrasted with those who threw large amounts into the coffers. "'I tell you the truth,' he said, 'this poor widow has put in more than all the others. All these people gave their gifts out of their wealth; but she out of her poverty put in all she had to live on'" (Luke 21:3–4). Another is seen in James's discussion of the treatment of the rich person and the poor person in the church (James 2:1–7). He is sharp in his condemnation of the favoritism shown to the rich man.

A final biblical text supporting this argument is Paul's discussion of the body, in 1 Corinthians 12. Here Paul notes that the various members of the human body have different functions, some of them more conspicuous than others, and that the same tends to be true within the church. In the latter case, there is a natural tendency to accord greater recognition and distinction to some persons than to others. This, says Paul, is not how it ought to be, however. He points out the practice of the more conspicuous parts feeling that they have no need of the less conspicuous, and then concludes his discussion by saying

> On the contrary, those parts of the body that seem to be weaker are indispensable, and the parts that we think are less honorable we treat with special honor. And the parts that are unpresentable are treated with special modesty, while our presentable parts need no special treatment. But God has combined the members of the body and has given greater honor to the parts that lacked it, so that there should be no division in the body, but that its parts should have equal concern for each other. If one part suffers, every part suffers with it; if one part is honored, every part rejoices with it. Now you are the body of Christ, and each one of you is a part of it (1 Cor. 12:22–27).

Sometimes this lack of awareness of the significance of each member of the body shows up in an emphasis on the pastor, to the neglect of giving credit to the lay members. Some churches are known as "Pastor X's church," and the pastor's name may appear on the church sign in letters equal in size to (or even larger than) the name of the congregation. This undermines the significance of the whole body. This is a natural reaction, for in society greater recognition is given to those who perform the more conspicuous roles. Quarterbacks, running backs, and pass receivers get more recognition for their football accomplishments than do the linemen, but they would have very little success without the blocking of those linemen.

This type of concern should carry over to all of our relationships to other believers, whether in a local congregation or elsewhere. One professor served for a time in a Christian educational institution where there were definite social classes: trustees, administrators, faculty, staff, students. Each group kept to themselves. Faculty and staff did not eat together, for example. The students, who were a rather selective group, both in terms of academic ability and socioeconomic class, ridiculed the maintenance staff in the campus publications and some even conveyed a sense of superiority to the faculty. Then he went to another institution, where the social structure was quite different. The founder of the school had enunciated as one of the principles on which the school should operate: "As nearly as possible the relationship between teacher and pupil shall be one of equality. There shall be only one master, but we are all brothers." Here there were no class barriers. In the lunchroom, professor, custodian, dean, student, secretary, could all be seen eating at the same table. Professors did not insist upon being referred as "Doctor," and were often addressed by first name. Their office doors were open, both figuratively and literally. After several years at that institution, he moved on to a third school, where professors were on a pedestal and were always referred to as "Doctor," but accustomed to the practice at the previous school, he operated more informally. One day his secretary said to him, "You know, you are the favorite professor of the secretaries in this building." Seeing his puzzled look, she explained, "It's because you talk to all of them, and you treat them as equals." Jesus told his disciples that they were not to be like the Pharisees, who "love the place of honor at banquets and the most important seats in the synagogues; they love to be greeted in the marketplaces and to have men call them 'Rabbi.' But you are not to be called 'Rabbi,' for you have only one Master and you are all brothers" (Matt. 23:6–8).

What is to be true in the relationship between individual believers should also apply to the relationship between congregations. In American society, we are impressed with size, and that often carries over to our appraisal of churches too. The model of what congregations should be is often the megachurch. To be sure, there are dimensions of programming quality that follow from the greater resources and economy of scale present in a larger congregation. And some churches are small because they are not making very good use of their resources and opportunities. Having said that, however, we should beware of despising the smaller congregation, or treating it as unimportant. Some churches have moved into the proximity of a sister congregation, not because more people overall would be reached (including those in the community they have left), but because such a move affords them a better opportunity to grow. What had been the means to the end of reaching more people now becomes the end in itself, for the growth of which more people are needed. In the process, little attention is given to the welfare of the other congregation. In fact, one pastor said to me, "Those little churches will be eaten up by the big churches, but that is a good thing, because they aren't doing the job anyway." It did not matter that there were some people whom his church would not and could not reach, and for that matter did not care to reach, who would not be reached because the other church was put out of business. Sometimes there is a competitiveness between churches, in which each seeks to reach a diminishing number of persons (middle-class whites, for example), much like whalers concentrating on a diminishing number of whales.

What we have said about the implication of understanding the internal relationships of the Trinity for individual Christians should apply here as well. The church that reflects the Triune God will be concerned for the needs of other congregations as well as for its own. It will share its resources where needed, rather than keeping them entirely for itself. I have seen dramatic instances of this, both positive and negative. One rather small congregation, located on the edge of an airport in a major metropolitan area and forced to sell their property, could well have reasoned that they needed the entire proceeds of the sale of the building to apply to the acquisition of new facilities. Yet they chose to give a tithe of those proceeds to their district and national denominational offices. On the other hand, one moderately large church brought in a consultant from a megachurch. His first recommendation was that they reduce their missionary giving, which they already felt was too small, in order to invest more of their resources in their local program. It can, of course, be argued that a stronger home base makes possible a more extensive outreach, but that might have been better accomplished by contributing to church planting. Sometimes even in the process of starting daughter churches, the mother church makes certain that they take a name that clearly identifies them as daughters of the mother church.

In families, there should be an application of the relationships that characterize the Triune God whose image we bear. Whether we are able to dictate from this doctrine the exact shape such a family structure would take, the Christian family should be concerned that each person be treated as important, and that their input into decisions be taken seriously.

Finally, within society we should be concerned to regard all human persons with respect, dignity, and value. Our society places very unequal values on people, often indicating those values by financial reward. In some cases there is a relationship between persons' contributions to society and their compensation. Is it really the case, however, that an outstanding athlete, or a media star, is worth 1,000 or 10,000 times what a teacher or a nurse is? Beyond that, however, the adulation attached to certain of the "beautiful people," the "superstars," suggests that the loss of one of them would be far more serious than that of a construction laborer or a checkout person.

This is not how it is, however, in the eyes of God, who according to Jesus is so concerned for each of us that he is like the shepherd, who with ninety-nine sheep in the fold, left them and went to seek the one lost sheep (Luke 15:3–7). The unselfish love of the members of the Trinity spills over into their love for their creatures, and should also be present in the lives of their human creatures.

Notes

Introduction

1. John Naisbitt and Patricia Aburdene, *Megatrends 2000: Ten New Directions for the 1990's* (New York: Avon, 1990), p. 297.

Chapter 1: *Is the Doctrine of the Trinity Biblical?*

1. Percival Gardner-Smith, *Saint John and the Synoptic Gospels* (Cambridge: Cambridge University Press, 1938).

2. Martin Hengel, *Acts and the History of Earliest Christianity* (Philadelphia: Fortress, 1979), pp. 3–34.

3. Royce Gordon Gruenler, *New Approaches to Jesus and the Gospels: A Phenomenological and Exegetical Study of Synoptic Christology* (Grand Rapids: Baker, 1982), p. 15.

4. Craig Blomberg, *The Historical Reliability of the Gospels* (Downers Grove, Ill.: InterVarsity, 1987), pp. 183–84.

5. F. F. Bruce, "The Dead Sea Scrolls and Early Christianity," *Bulletin of the John Rylands Library* 49 (Autumn 1966): 81.

6. W. F. Albright, *The Archaeology of Palestine*, rev. ed. (Baltimore: Penguin, 1956), pp. 242–49.

7. C. H. Dodd, *Historical Tradition in the Fourth Gospel* (Cambridge: Cambridge University Press, 1963), p. 128. For a summary of the entire argument and conclusions, see pp. 423–32.

8. John A. T. Robinson, *Redating the New Testament* (Philadelphia: Westminster, 1976), pp. 9–10; Bo Reicke, "Synoptic Problems on the Destruction of Jerusalem," in *Studies in New Testament and Early Christian Literature: Essays in Honor of Allen P. Wikgren* (supplement to *Novum Testamentum* 33), ed. David E. Aune (Leiden: Brill, 1972), p. 121.

9. Philo, *On the Creation of the World* 24.

10. *Berakhot,* 9:1, VI, A–G. *The Talmud of the Land of Israel* (Chicago: University of Chicago Press, 1989), 1:307–8.

11. C. G. Montefiore and H. Loewe, *A Rabbinic Anthology* (New York: Schocken, 1974), p. 664.

12. Arthur W. Wainwright, *The Trinity in the New Testament* (London: SPCK, 1962), p. 25.

13. *On the Confusion of Languages* 33–34.

14. Philo, *A Treatise on the Life of the Wise Man Made Perfect by Instruction, or, on the Unwritten Law, That is to Say, on Abraham,* 24–28.

15. *The Targum of Isaiah,* ed. J. F. Stenning (Oxford: Clarendon, 1949), pp. 22–23.

16. For a summary of this discussion, see Murray J. Harris, *Jesus as God: The New Testament Use of* Theos *in Reference to Jesus* (Grand Rapids: Baker, 1992), pp. 57–71, 301–13.

17. Vincent Taylor, *The Person of Christ* (London: Macmillan, 1958), p. 150.

18. Ibid., p. 147.

Chapter 2: *Does the Doctrine of the Trinity Make Sense?*

1. Tertullian, *De praescriptione haereticorum* 7. Note, however, that Tertullian vigorously defended the doctrine of the Trinity against false views.

2. Søren Kierkegaard, *Concluding Unscientific Postscript* (Princeton, N.J.: Princeton University Press, 1941), p. 189.

3. George Santayana, *The Life of Reason or the Phases of Human Progress,* 2nd ed. (New York: Scribner's, 1936), vol. 1, p. 284; one-vol. rev. ed. (New York: Scribner's, 1953), p. 82.

4. Epiphanius, *Against Eighty Heresies* 55.9.

5. Eusebius, *Ecclesiastical History* 7.30.10.

6. Jaroslav Pelikan, *The Christian Tradition: A History of the Development of Doctrine* (Chicago: University of Chicago Press, 1971), 1:176.

7. Eusebius, *Ecclesiastical History* 7.28.2; Adolf Harnack, *History of Dogma* (New York: Dover, 1961), 3:38–39.

8. Hippolytus, *Against Noetus* 1; Tertullian, *Against Praxeas* 5, 7, 10.

9. Athanasius, *Orations Against the Arians* 1.5, 9; Arius, *Epistle to Alexander* (in Athanasius, *On the Synods of Ariminum and Seleucia* 16).

10. Epiphanius of Salamis, *Against Eighty Heresies* 73.13.1.

11. Edward Gibbon, *The Decline and Fall of the Roman Empire* (New York: Peter Fenelon Collier, 1899), 2:252.

12. Daniel Day Williams, *What Present-Day Theologians Are Thinking* (New York: Harper, 1952).

13. Donald Baillie, *God Was in Christ*. (New York: Scribner's, 1948).

14. E.g., Leonardo Boff, *Trinity and Society* (Maryknoll, N.Y.: Orbis, 1988); Jürgen Moltmann, *The Trinity and the Kingdom: The Doctrine of God* (San Francisco: Harper & Row, 1981).

15. "Katie and Eilish," *Discovery Journal* (the Discovery television channel), February 1993.

Chapter 3: *Does the Doctrine of the Trinity Make Any Difference?*

1. Immanuel Kant, *Der Streit der Fakultäten* (Hamburg: Felix Meiner, 1975 [Philosophische Bibliothek, Band 252]), p. 34.

2. Karl Rahner, *The Trinity* (New York: Herder and Herder, 1970), pp. 10–11.

3. Ibid., p. 11.

4 Raimundo Panikkar, *The Trinity and the Religious Experience of Man* (New York: Orbis, 1973), p. viii.

5. Ibid., pp. 11–40.

6. Geoffrey Wainwright, *Doxology*, pp. 92–93.

7. Arthur W. Wainwright, *The Trinity in the New Testament* (London: S.P.C.K., 1962), p. 228.

8. Leonard Hodgson, *The Doctrine of the Trinity* (New York: Scribners, 1944), p. 232.

9. *On the Holy Spirit* 73.

10. Arthur Wainwright, *The Trinity in the New Testament*, p. 229.

11. *The Acts of Thomas* 27.

12. *On the Holy Spirit* 10.24.

13. Ibid., 29.75.

14. Ibid., 29.73.

15. Geoffrey Bromiley, "Eternal Generation," in *Evangelical Dictionary of Theology*, ed. Walter A. Elwell (Grand Rapids: Baker, 1984), p. 368.

16. Ibid.

17. Benjamin Breckenridge Warfield, "The Biblical Doctrine of the Trinity," in *Biblical and Theological Studies,* ed. Samuel G. Craig (Philadelphia: Presbyterian & Reformed, 1952), p. 50.

18. Ibid.

19. Royce Gordon Gruenler, *The Trinity in the Gospel of John: A Thematic Commentary on the Fourth Gospel* (Grand Rapids: Baker, 1986).

Scripture Index

Subject Index

Galatians, structure of, 38–39
Gibbon, Edward, 52
God
   deity of, 19
   Old Testament plurals and,
     31–33
   three-in-oneness of, 29–31,
     62
   in Acts, 37
   in the baptismal formula,
     34
   in the Book of Hebrews,
     36–37
   in John's writings, 39–42
   in the Old Testament,
     31–34
   in Paul's writings, 34–36,
     37–39
   in Peter's writings, 36
   unity of, 18–19, 33–34
Gospels, dating of, 26
Gruenler, Royce, 89

Hinduism, 14, 76
Hodgson, Leonard, 81
Holy Spirit. *See also* prayer, to
    the Holy Spirit; worship,
    and the Holy Spirit
   deity of, 26–29
   eternality of, 28
   indwelling of the believer, 27
   in the Old Testament, 29, 65
   omnipotence of, 27–28
   omniscience of, 27
homoiousios, 52
homotimos, 82
homoousious, 52, 82, 83
hypostasis, 54

idolatry, 18, 19

image of God, 53, 84–85
incarnation, the, 60, 70
   as a model, 89
   and the problem of evil, 74
   influence Christology, 55–56
Islam, 14, 76

Jehovah's Witnesses, 14, 51–52
Jerusalem Talmud, 32
Jesus
   conception of, 27
   deity of, 19–26
   preexistence of, 54–55
   self-understanding, 20–22
John, Gospel of
   dating, 25–26
   and the Dead Sea Scrolls, 24
   geographical references in,
     24–25
   John Rylands fragment of, 25
   reliability, 23–25
   and the Synoptics, 23, 24, 25
Judaism, 14, 76
   monotheism of, 18, 47
justification, 35, 38–39

Kant, Immanuel, 70
kenosis, 87
Kierkegaard, Søren, 44
King James Version, 29–30

"Lord, We Are Able," 49
Lord's Prayer, 77
Luke, Gospel of, geographical
    references in, 24

Mark, Gospel of, 25
messiah, Old Testament expec-
    tations, 19–20

modalism, 45, 49–50
morphē, 20

New Age religion, 14

On the Holy Spirit (Basil of Caesarea), 82
Origen, 81–82
orthodoxy, 73

Panikaar, Raimundo, 76
pantheism, 57
Papias, 32
Pelikan, Jaroslav, 48
perichoresis, 57, 59–60, 64, 78
persona, 54
Philo, 32, 33
plural of majesty, 31
pluralism, 76
pneumati, 80
pragmatism, 71
prayer, 77–79
    to "all three," 78
    to the "Father only," 77–78
    to the Holy Spirit, 79–84
    to Jesus, 78–79

Rahner, Karl, 70
Rauschenbusch, Walter, 73
redemption, 65. *See also* atonement
regeneration, 27, 28, 83, 84
relevance, 71–72
Robinson, John A. T., 23–24, 26
Romans, structure of, 37–38

salvation, 15
sanctification, 64
Santayana, George, 47
schēma, 20

Schleiermacher, Friedrich, 73
Scripture
    as Christian's source of authority, 17
    and inspiration, 28–29, 83
semi-Arianism, 52
separation, of human persons
    by differing experiences, 59–60
    by physical bodies, 59
    by self-preoccupation, 60
Shema, 18, 33
Smith, W. Robertson, 48
social gospel, 73
son, meaning in Hebrew culture, 89
suffering, 36

Targums
    Jerusalem, 32
    Onkelos, 32
    Palestinian, 32, 33
Taylor, Vincent, 42
Tertullian, 44
textual criticism
theology
    "official," 70
    "unofficial," 70–71
Trinity. *See also* God, three-in-oneness of
    analogies for
        authorized representative, 56
        clones, 55
        egg, 53
        father/son, 54
        human personality, 53–54
        joint tenancy, 56
        multiple roles, 55
        trousers, 53
        partnership, 56

Millard J. Erickson is Distinguished Professor of Theology at Baylor University's Truett Seminary. He is a leading evangelical spokesman with numerous volumes to his credit, including *Christian Theology, Introducing Christian Doctrine, God in Three Persons, The Word Became Flesh, God the Father Almighty,* and *Postmodernizing the Faith.*